THE

WHERE THE WORLD MEETS TO PRAY

Susan Hibbins
UK Editor

INTERDENOMINATIONAL
INTERNATIONAL
INTERRACIAL

33 LANGUAGES
Multiple formats are available in some languages

The Bible Reading Fellowship
15 The Chambers, Vineyard
Abingdon OX14 3FE
brf.org.uk

The Bible Reading Fellowship (BRF) is a Registered Charity (233280)

ISBN 978 0 85746 783 6

Acknowledgements

Scripture quotations marked NRSV are taken from The New Revised Standard Version of the Bible, Anglicised Edition, copyright © 1989, 1995 by the Division of Christian Education of the National Council of the Churches of Christ in the USA. Used by permission. All rights reserved.

Scripture quotations marked NIV are taken from The Holy Bible, New International Version (Anglicised edition) copyright © 1979, 1984, 2011 by Biblica. Used by permission of Hodder & Stoughton Publishers, an Hachette UK company. All rights reserved. 'NIV' is a registered trademark of Biblica. UK trademark number 1448790.

Extracts marked KJV are from the Authorised Version of the Bible (The King James Bible), the rights in which are vested in the Crown, are reproduced by permission of the Crown's Patentee, Cambridge University Press.

Extracts from CEB copyright © 2011 by Common English Bible.

Where scripture verse references are not followed by an initialism, the quotation is taken from the same version as that of the quotation at the top of the page.

A catalogue record for this book is available from the British Library

Printed by Gutenberg Press, Tarxien, Malta

How to use *The Upper Room*

The Upper Room is ideal in helping us spend a quiet time with God each day. Each daily entry is based on a passage of scripture, and is followed by a meditation and prayer. Each person who contributes a meditation to the magazine seeks to relate their experience of God in a way that will help those who use *The Upper Room* every day.

Here are some guidelines to help you make best use of *The Upper Room*:

1 Read the passage of scripture. It is a good idea to read it more than once, in order to have a fuller understanding of what it is about and what you can learn from it.
2 Read the meditation. How does it relate to your own experience? Can you identify with what the writer has outlined from their own experience or understanding?
3 Pray the written prayer. Think about how you can use it to relate to people you know, or situations that need your prayers today.
4 Think about the contributor who has written the meditation. Some users of the *The Upper Room* include this person in their prayers for the day.
5 Meditate on the 'Thought for the day' and the 'Prayer focus', perhaps using them again as the focus for prayer or direction for action.

Why is it important to have a daily quiet time? Many people will agree that it is the best way of keeping in touch every day with the God who sustains us, and who sends us out to do his will and show his love to the people we encounter each day. Meeting with God in this way reassures us of his presence with us, helps us to discern his will for us and makes us part of his worldwide family of Christian people through our prayers.

I hope that you will be encouraged as you use the magazine regularly as part of your daily devotions, and that God will richly bless you as you read his word and seek to learn more about him.

Susan Hibbins
UK Editor

CAN YOU HELP?

Here at BRF, we're always looking for ways to promote the practice of daily Bible reading, and we would like to ask for your help in spreading the word about this valuable resource.

Can I ask you to spread the word about the usefulness of *The Upper Room* in aiding daily meditation and prayer? This could be among your friends and contacts, or at any events in which you might be involved, such as church or a Bible study group, or a conference, special service, retreat or workshop.

We would really value your help, and we'll happily send you some sample copies if you can use them. Just let me know how many you would like and I'll arrange for them to be sent to you. If you wish you can email me at **susan. hibbins@brf.org.uk**.

If you're active on social media, we can supply cover graphics for use on Twitter, Facebook and so on, and we can also supply information packs to churches and groups if you pass on any requests to me.

Thank you in advance for helping us to publicise our Bible reading notes.

Susan Hibbins
UK Editor, The Upper Room

Faithful waiting

God remembered Noah, all those alive, and all the animals with him in the ark. God sent a wind over the earth so that the waters receded.
Genesis 8:1 (CEB)

The story of Noah and the flood is a familiar one. I often hear this story recounted as one of both God's anger with humanity and God's covenant with Noah. But it is also a story of faithful waiting. When Noah follows God's command to build an ark, there is no sign of rain. The people around him think he is crazy, but Noah persists, patiently following God's instructions. When the waters rise, Noah, his family and all the creatures of the earth enter the ark. What must have been long and terrifying days and nights of waiting begin. Scripture does not tell us what Noah does or thinks while waiting for the storm to cease and the waters to recede, but we know that 'Noah did everything the Lord commanded him' (Genesis 7:5). Noah followed God's leadng, and God remembered Noah.

Waiting faithfully is always an act of hope and trust in God. Many writers in this issue describe experiences of waiting, seeking God's guidance and faithfully holding on to the hope that God's power and love for us provide. These stories of faithful waiting encourage me and remind me that God sends others to support us in our waiting and, most important of all, that God remembers us and is with us as we wait. As you seek God's guidance and wait in the coming months, I pray that these stories will give you courage, hope and an opportunity to draw closer to God.

Lindsay L. Gray
Editorial Director, The Upper Room

Where the world meets to pray

Editions of *The Upper Room* daily devotional guide are printed in:

- **Hong Kong** (Chinese, Chinese/English)
- **Japan** (Japanese, English)
- **Korea** (Korean, Korean/English, and Korean/English/Japanese)

Korea

Last year *The Upper Room* celebrated 80 years of publishing in Korea! Publishing partners from all over Asia gathered in Seoul for a celebration and training event to commemorate the occasion.

Gifts to the international editions of *The Upper Room* help the world meet to pray.
upperroom.org/gift

Photos courtesy of the Revd Thomas Kim, UMNS

The Editor writes...

When I go for my daily walk, I pass by two adjoining areas of riverbank. One is owned by our town council and is bordered by a neat row of railings and an open gate. Inside there is a picnic table and bench and another seat by the river. I sometimes sit and look at the trees swaying in the breeze, the sunlight flickering on the water and the numerous ducks, moorhens and coots that swim in and out of the reeds. Sometimes a swan floats by. It is a lovely oasis in our town, inviting people in to pause and be refreshed.

Next to this area is a privately owned garden. There is a strong padlocked gate across the entrance, and a stern 'Private – Keep Out' notice forbids you to enter. Inside there are overgrown shrubs and bedraggled flowerbeds; the grass is long and uncared for, and an old garden bench stands forlorn and dilapidated in one corner. The contrast between the two areas could not be greater.

I thought about how different a place can be when it is open to people, cared for and made welcoming. Then I thought about our own hearts. We may keep a 'private' notice on the door to our hearts, which keeps both Jesus and other people from entering. Sometimes we find it hard to open up to others, fearing their reactions to our inmost feelings. There are things that we hide in the corners of our hearts, even from Jesus, hoping they will never be discovered. Our hearts become choked and shadowed, and God's love cannot get in and help us clear up the mess.

In John 14:23 Jesus says to his disciples, 'Anyone who loves me will obey my teaching. My Father will love them, and we will come to them and make our home with them' (NIV). In obeying Jesus we are opening our hearts and making them fit places for him and his Father to dwell. He helps us to clear away what is overgrown, get rid of the clutter and make what is there fresh and new, so it is a pleasant place to be. And, in doing so, we also extend a welcome to others, ready to share with them what Jesus has done for us.

I pray that my heart, and yours, may be open to the sunshine of God's presence as you read this edition of *The Upper Room*.

Susan Hibbins
UK Editor

The Bible readings are selected with great care, and we urge you to include the suggested reading in your devotional time.

Come near

Read Psalm 113

Come near to God, and he will come near to you.
James 4:8 (CEB)

Recently my children and grandchildren came to stay for a week at my house. I noticed that we each had habits and activities that we did throughout the day. Some of us checked our phones frequently. Some went outside for fresh air. The grandchildren kept getting out more toys. Some wanted snacks to eat, and I spent more time than usual washing up.

Noticing these patterns made me think that if we were to read our Bible or pray as much as we do other things throughout the day, we could draw nearer and nearer to God. I decided that I would pray whenever I did the washing-up. I suggested to my children and grandchildren that they say a quick prayer every time they reach for a snack, for their phone or for a toy or when they go outside for a breath of fresh air. Scripture reminds us that when we pray continually and draw near to God, he will draw near to us.

Prayer: *Dear God, help us to keep you in our thoughts throughout the day so that we may draw nearer to you. In Jesus' name, we pray. Amen*

Thought for the day: Today I will make prayer a part of my routine.

Annie Gipson (Missouri, US)

Entertaining angels

Read Genesis 18:1–5
[Jesus] poured water into a basin and began to wash his disciples'
feet, drying them with the towel that was wrapped round him.
John 13:5 (NIV)

During a period of hot weather, a friend gave me some foot soak crystals and foot lotion. What a practical and welcome gift!

Foot washing in hot countries was a common courtesy performed by a host (or his servant) when welcoming someone to his home. The first recorded foot-washing incident in the Bible is the story of three men visiting Abraham. It was the hottest part of the day, but Abraham hurried to meet the men, bowed and asked that they would break their journey so that he could serve them.

Years later, to the astonishment of his disciples, Jesus – their Lord and master – bent down to wash their feet. Abraham, the great patriarch; Jesus, the Saviour of the world: both are examples of servant leadership.

Visitors to your home might be surprised if you greeted them with a towel and said, 'Let me wash your feet.' The principle is to look to others' comfort, with grace, kindness, thoughtfulness and generosity. By the grace of God we can learn to live generously, giving of ourselves in loving service – whatever the weather.

Prayer: *Lord, give me the humility to serve others in whatever way is appropriate, just as you serve me with generous love. Amen*

Thought for the day: How can I serve someone today?

Pam Pointer (Wiltshire, England)

Never alone

Read Luke 11:5–13

Ask and it will be given to you; seek and you will find; knock and the door will be opened to you. For everyone who asks receives; the one who seeks finds; and to the one who knocks, the door will be opened.
Luke 11:9–10 (NIV)

After my husband of more than 64 years died, I found myself living alone for the first time in my 80-plus years. It was truly an adjustment. I often caught myself saying something aloud and then answering myself. I was so starved for companionship that if I ever was with others, I would just chatter on – so glad that I was finally able to discuss daily events and activities. I was definitely seeking the 'new normal' in my life.

I found consolation in my church, my friends and my writing, but I still felt a void in my life. One day I began reading *The Upper Room* and soon discovered a kinship with others. The life experiences of the writers motivated me to draw closer to the Lord, my true friend and Saviour. I now know that I am not living alone, for God is with me at all times to talk to and to enrich and inspire my life with unconditional love.

Connection with God gives me the strength to get up each morning with the resolve to challenge myself in new ways, to ask myself: how can I fulfil God's purpose for me and help others to see that they are never alone? Hand in hand with the Lord, I'll find the answer.

Prayer: *Dear Lord, thank you for wrapping us in your love. Help us to grow in faith so that others will see through us your abiding care. Amen*

Thought for the day: God's grace and Spirit are always with me.

Lois E. Wilson (Ohio, US)

Thanks be to God

Read Romans 7:14–25
Thanks be to God, who delivers me through Jesus Christ our Lord!
Romans 7:25 (NIV)

When my daughter asked for apple pie, I picked out three perfect-looking green apples to make it with. However, after peeling and cutting one of the apples, I found that it was completely rotten inside.

At times I feel exactly like that: nice and presentable on the outside but a disaster inside. Despite my best efforts to be an excellent wife and a patient mother, the apostle Paul's words ring true: 'I do not do the good I want to do, but the evil I do not want to do – this I keep on doing' (Romans 7:19). I have been a Christian for decades, and I delight in God's word. I admit that God's ways are better than my own. Still, I often assume that what I want is most important or that I deserve what my heart desires – straight away.

I wonder if it is possible to escape this inner battle. The Bible teaches that as long as we live, we will struggle with sin. But the apostle Paul also writes, 'Thanks be to God, who delivers me through Jesus Christ our Lord!' (Romans 7:25). Jesus always fights my battles with me. Whenever temptation presents itself, I know I can cry for help and try to imitate Jesus. He promised to deliver us, and we can count on his word!

Prayer: *Dear God, help us to guard our hearts from evil. Thank you for delivering us through Jesus Christ, who helps us in our daily battles. Amen*

Thought for the day: Although sin abounds, God's mercy overcomes.

Marcela Nwanosike (Lincolnshire, England)

A forgotten inscription

Read Philippians 2:12–18

There is no one who can deliver from my hand; I work and who can hinder it?
Isaiah 43:13 (NRSV)

When I was young, my grandmother gave me a small black Bible with this inscription: 'Dear Greg: This little Bible is your very first one, so keep it nice. You are getting big so pretty soon you will be able to read it. I pray the dear Lord will keep you under His wing and help you to grow up to be a strong, healthy boy and that you will go often to the Bible for strength and courage as you go through life – Gram, October 31, 1968.'

I soon forgot the inscription, but as I grew I matured in my faith. Then that Bible was replaced with a larger one.

During a recent time of prayer, I saw my forgotten Bible on a shelf. I read the inscription and I could hear my grandma's voice again. I was overcome with emotion. How could I tell her how God had faithfully answered her prayer and what a wonderful example of Christ she was to me?

Grandma's prayer and Christian witness continue to be evident in my life. I go to the Bible for strength and courage and God has never failed to provide. Today as we pray, each of us can thank God for the Christian influences in our lives.

Prayer: *Dear God, thank you for providing for our needs and giving us Christian mentors in our lives. Help us to grow in our relationship with you. Amen*

Thought for the day: In what ways can I offer encouragement to new Christians?

Greg Romano (Indiana, US)

Dirty dishes

Read 1 John 1:5–10

If we confess our sins, [God] is faithful and just and will forgive us our sins and purify us from all unrighteousness.
1 John 1:9 (NIV)

When a plate goes unwashed after a meal, it will probably remain in the sink overnight. Because the food dries firmly on the plate, it takes much longer to clean than one that is washed immediately after a meal.

The unwashed plate makes me think about the things in our lives that need cleansing. Maybe we need to pray for forgiveness or for help forgiving others; maybe immorality, injustice or other sins are harming our relationships with others and with God.

Much like washing up, the best thing for our lives is to acknowledge the dirt immediately and not postpone action for the future; waiting only makes it more difficult to change. But even when we leave dirt in our lives long enough for it to stick, forgiveness is a powerful cleanser. God asks that we forgive others, and he forgives us – he cleanses us from sin through the power of Jesus' blood.

Prayer: *Forgiving God, thank you for cleansing us from our sin. Help us to show your forgiveness to others and to be quick to wash the dirt from our lives and our relationships. Amen*

Thought for the day: Because God has forgiven me, I am free to forgive others.

Conny Hedengren (Jonkoping, Sweden)

Ordinary heroes

Read 1 Corinthians 1:26–31

God chose what the world considers low-class and low-life – what is considered to be nothing – to reduce what is considered to be something to nothing.
1 Corinthians 1:28 (CEB)

In popular literature, plays and poetry, the common people often have unimportant roles while the exalted parts go to kings, princes and princesses.

But the New Testament flips that perception. In God's story, the common people take centre stage. It is not a king's eloquent decree that made Jesus stop, but rather the blind beggar who desperately called out his name. As others rushed by this man, Jesus saw his value. The widow who donated two copper coins is a heroine (see Mark 12:41–44). Jesus did not ignore the common people or portray them as buffoons.

In the gospels, we read about the nameless in the stories of the prodigal son and the paralytic who was healed. What a contrast to other stories of kings and rulers! We like to read about celebrities and people who lead glamorous lives, but God often does the opposite of what we expect. He prefers to focus on ordinary people and how they become quiet heroes through loving acts of faith – and he invites us to do the same.

Prayer: *God of all people, help us to look beyond earthly success. Open our eyes to see the value of all people, just as you do. Amen*

Thought for the day: God exalts those who act with faith.

Bob LaForge (New Jersey, US)

Contentment

Read Zephaniah 3:14–20

The Lord your God… will rejoice over you with singing.
Zephaniah 3:17 (CEB)

I loved to rock my children and grandchildren when they were young. My youngest daughter always enjoyed snuggling in my arms; with her many health concerns she often felt ill and needed comfort. I would wrap her in her favourite blanket, rock her and softly sing 'Jesus Loves Me'. She would settle down contentedly.

Years later I looked after my infant grandson, Nathaniel, one evening each week. After I had changed him and prepared his evening bottle, I would wrap him in a blanket, rock him, feed him and softly sing 'Jesus Loves Me' to him. He would relax and snuggle contentedly, soothed by his grandma singing over him.

I think of these two generations of babies whenever I read today's quoted verse. God loves each one of us more than I could ever love my children and grandchildren. I feel overwhelmed when I realise how much the God of the universe delights in me. He sings over all of us and wants us to come, curl up and find comfort.

Prayer: *Dear God, thank you for loving us completely. Help us to remember how much you love and want to comfort us. Amen*

Thought for the day: I can feel safe in God's comforting embrace.

Carol Harrison (Saskatchewan, Canada)

Full access

Read Hebrews 4:12–16

Through faith in [Christ Jesus our Lord] we may approach God with freedom and confidence.
Ephesians 3:12 (NIV)

Three days of heavy rain left our area saturated with overflowing streams, causing full drainage ditches, soggy gardens and flooded roads between the hills. 'Road Closed' signs blocked the streets, causing drivers to seek alternative routes. When I tried to get to the main road, I found it barricaded, so that I had to turn around. The detour increased my frustration in getting where I needed to go.

Gripping the steering wheel, I realised I had a choice – to let the annoyance of the detour irritate me or to pray that God would calm my mind in spite of the road closures. Then I thought: 'When I pray, nothing ever stands as an obstacle. I have full access to God at any time!'

Jesus Christ is the way to God (John 14:6), and through him, we can draw near to God with confidence (Hebrews 4:16). We have many ways to connect with God, such as through prayer, reading the Bible, worshipping with others, listening to Christian music and serving his people. God never puts up a 'Road Closed' sign. When we approach with sincere hearts, he will receive us.

Prayer: *Dear Lord, thank you for reminders that you are always with us. Amen*

Thought for the day: Through prayer, I can reach God at any time and from any place.

Nancy Kay Grace (Arkansas, US)

Abundant peace

Read Philippians 4:1–8

Are any among you suffering? They should pray. Are any cheerful?
They should sing songs of praise.
James 5:13 (NRSV)

When our four-year-old son was diagnosed with leukaemia, my wife and I dropped everything so that we could spend all our time with him at the local children's hospital. We struggled to keep a brave outward appearance as we dealt with a barrage of tests and procedures and meetings with doctors, family and chaplains, but inside we were shell-shocked.

One night, however, I awoke to a palpable feeling of reassurance and warmth. In place of all my worry and fear lingered the most complete peace I have ever felt.

From that point on, every time we took our son to his monthly checkup and chemo clinic, we read chapter four of Philippians. Admittedly, it was always a struggle not to worry, but still I felt God's presence. Throughout our son's three-and-a-half-year chemotherapy treatment, we continually made known our requests to God.

Our son is now 13 years old, and he does most of the things a normal 13-year-old boy does. Just as we did that night, we continue to experience God's presence in every one of our annual survivor-clinic visits. God has been there for all of it, offering us hope, loving-kindness and abundant peace.

Prayer: *Compassionate God, send peace to all those who worry over their health and the health of their loved ones. Fill us with peace that banishes our fears and anxieties. Amen*

Thought for the day: In the midst of trouble, I am surrounded by God's peace.

Robert Harris (Georgia, US)

Life in community

Read Acts 2:42–47

They devoted themselves to the apostles' teaching and to fellowship, to the breaking of bread and to prayer.
Acts 2:42 (NIV)

As I rushed to the front door one Tuesday morning, my husband stopped me. 'Have you seen this?' he asked, pointing to the television screen. I glanced over my shoulder and saw a plane crashing into the World Trade Center. 'Oh, that's awful!' Because 15 women were waiting for me to lead Bible study, I didn't have time to think more about it and rushed out of the door.

But when I arrived, the group was discussing what they had heard or seen that morning. Our fears and concerns escalated with news that the Pentagon had also been hit. When I tried to start the lesson, no one could focus. So we went into the church to pray. We knew so little that it was hard to form the words, but it felt right to be kneeling at an altar, in community with other children of God, on that day – 11 September 2001.

After Jesus was physically no longer with them, the early church had only one another to rely on. Luke's joy is evident as he writes about their life in community. They ate, learned and worshipped together. Our faith is strengthened by others as they encourage us, love us and hold us accountable. The early church is a model of what God intended – that we travel through our journey of faith and life in community.

Prayer: *Heavenly Father, thank you for placing faithful Christians in our lives to support and guide us on our journeys. Amen*

Thought for the day: My community strengthens my faith.

Marcy Farr (Texas, US)

Called to obey

Read 1 Samuel 15:1–25

Samuel replied [to Saul]: 'Does the Lord delight in burnt offerings and sacrifices as much as in obeying the Lord? To obey is better than sacrifice, and to heed is better than the fat of rams.'
1 Samuel 15:22 (NIV)

As I pushed my baby in his pram down the road, I prayed with each step. I was in the middle of another bout of anxiety and depression as a result of an illness I'd had for eleven years. While housebound and isolated from others for the previous two years, I had tearfully prayed every night that I would make friends. Also, I had been agonising over how I was going to give my new baby a happy and active life. So when I felt God nudging me to go to my church's morning service for the first time in nine years, I was filled with fear.

For others, this may seem like a small challenge, but the Lord knew how hard it was for me. Yet this small step of obedience changed my life forever. As a result of going to church that day, I was introduced to a house group run by a lovely young couple with a young boy the same age as mine.

Now I have a wonderful community around me who support me and cheer me on and with whom I pray and worship God – and my little boy has a best friend to grow up with. What a lesson I've learned about being open to God's leading!

Prayer: *Dear Father, thank you for your word and for guiding us through our days. Help us to listen for your voice and to obey you even when we don't understand why. Amen*

Thought for the day: Today, in small things and in great, I will look for the ways God is calling me to obey.

Hannah Blavins (Derbyshire, England)

Fishing for people

Read Matthew 4:18–22

'Come, follow me,' Jesus said, 'and I will send you out to fish for people.'
Matthew 4:19 (NIV)

Recently I took my five-year-old grandson on a fishing trip. He was very excited at the thought of catching a fish, even though he had no idea what he would do with it once he caught it. After I had set up his fishing rod, he was determined to bait his own hook and make the cast all by himself; but he still needed me to guide him.

His enthusiasm reminded me of how excited we are when we first accept Christ as our Saviour. We can't wait to share the gospel and 'fish for people'. Sometimes, like my grandson, we want to do everything all by ourselves because we think that we've got it all worked out. But our heavenly Father knows better and puts people in our lives to help us to grow and mature so that we can effectively serve.

After several casts and no fish, my grandson's excitement waned and his focus turned to other things. This reminded me of how it is with us as we serve God. Sometimes when things don't work out exactly the way we think they should, we can become distracted or frustrated. That's when those God-appointed mentors can help us stay focused. In so doing, we draw closer to them, closer to God and closer to those we are serving in God's name.

Prayer: *Dear God, our guide, thank you for watching over us and putting others in our lives to help us grow and mature in faith. Amen*

Thought for the day: With God's help, I can share my faith with others.

W. Leon McBride (Georgia, US)

Freedom

Read Psalm 119:44–48
I will always obey your law, forever and ever. I will walk about in freedom, for I have sought out your precepts.
Psalm 119:44–45 (NIV)

When I walk our dog Oliver at the park without his lead, he loves to run ahead, sniffing the trees and chasing the squirrels. Giving him the freedom to enjoy the park on his own makes me happy. However, I keep a look-out for other dog-walkers. When I see one in the distance, I call Oliver back to me to put him on his lead until we are alone again.

I am always struck by Oliver's quick and happy obedience when I call him back. He knows his freedom is going to be curtailed; yet he still comes eagerly to my feet. Only because I know I can count on his quick obedience am I able to allow him off the lead at all.

In Oliver's obedience I see a lesson for my relationship to my heavenly Father. Just as my commands seem to limit Oliver's freedom, so God's commands sometimes feel restrictive. And yet, his commands are for my good. Through them, I will be able to fully enjoy the life he has given me. Still, I have to ask myself: 'Am I as quick and cheerful in my obedience to God as Oliver is to me? Or when God calls me to obedience, do I delay and sulk at having to be put on a lead?' I hope I can match Oliver's enthusiasm when God gives me a command.

Prayer: *Dear God, help us today to trust you enough to obey you quickly and cheerfully in all that you ask. Help us to remember that obeying you gives us freedom. Amen*

Thought for the day: Today I will strive to cheerfully obey God's commands.

Diana Allor (Michigan, US)

Wise counsel

Read James 1:2–6

Is not wisdom found among the aged? Does not long life bring understanding? To God belong wisdom and power; counsel and understanding are his.

Job 12:12–13 (NIV)

Since I turned 70, I have become short-tempered. I feel worthless when God seems to ignore my wish to serve the kingdom. I also feel hopeless when social inequities such as nepotism, cronyism, favouritism and other injustices spread over my country. From time to time I feel miserable and lonely. When these feelings arise, I wonder whether my relationship with God is still vital and intimate. I forget the past and murmur about what God is doing for me now.

In my youth, I felt that God loved my unique personality, honest prayers and even my raw emotions. He rescued me when I narrowly missed being killed in combat. I survived two car accidents. After that, God surprised me with a new career that would sustain me for the rest of my working life. As I arduously sought after success, he sometimes slowed down my pace, which definitely worked for my good. After retirement, when I worried about my small income, God gave me peace and rest.

Remembering all this, I decided to focus on building up patience and endurance. As a result, I am once again giving thanks for the spiritual wisdom and understanding God has given me and for peace and joy in the Holy Spirit. I now see that God has never stopped being faithful in my life.

Prayer: *Gracious God, when we feel depressed, help us to count our blessings and seek your wisdom and counsel. Amen*

Thought for the day: God offers wise counsel in every season of my life.

Young Chae Chung (Seoul, South Korea)

The gift of peace

Read Psalm 16:5–11

I keep my eyes always on the Lord. With him at my right hand, I shall not be shaken. Therefore my heart is glad and my tongue rejoices; my body also will rest secure.
Psalm 16:8–9 (NIV)

When I was seven years old, my life changed drastically and forever. Until then, I had been very close to my father. One night, suddenly and unexpectedly, he passed away – leaving me feeling lost and alone. After his death, things were very hard for my family, causing us to feel as if we were in a dark pit we could not get out of.

As the years passed, I was constantly scared of the future and would choose fear over joy of any sort. But when I realised that fear had become my closest friend, I knew I had a problem. One night, as I felt completely broken and afraid, I decided to ask the Lord for guidance in reading the Bible. By the grace of God, I immediately opened up to Psalm 16.

With tears of thankfulness, I gradually started to find peace in the comforting words encouraging us to rejoice because the God of the universe is at our right hand. I read that our souls dwell securely in a God who will never forsake us – even in our darkest hour.

The peace of God can conquer anything. Simply reading the Bible can change a heart of fear to a heart of joy, full of the most profound spiritual peace.

Prayer: *Heavenly Father, thank you for loving us and giving us peace through the reading of your word. Help us never to grow weary in trusting you. Amen*

Thought for the day: God has given us the Bible to bring peace to our souls.

Lydia Masters (Texas, US)

Answered prayers

Read Matthew 7:7–11

[Jesus replied to the disciples,] 'If you believe, you will receive whatever you ask for in prayer.'
Matthew 21:22 (NIV)

After retiring as CEO of a public company, I missed my job's challenges and activity. To help fill the vacuum, I turned to prayer – asking for guidance in serving God with my new abundance of free time. Then, during an Easter sermon, God inspired me to create bookmarks for prisoners. The purpose of the bookmarks is to provide comfort and motivate the inmates to seek faith in Christ by reading several scripture references as well as a concise summary of Christian beliefs. To date, 187,000 of these bookmarks have been distributed and well received in 343 prisons all over the country. Clearly, God has answered my prayer, although I had not expected to be led in this direction.

God does hear and answer our prayers. Sometimes, the answers may be exactly what we expected. Others are subtle and easily overlooked, as we focus solely on our own expectations. Some we recognise only when we look back after the passage of time. Others may seem to remain unanswered altogether. In every situation, we can be assured that God wants the very best for us.

Prayer: *Dear Lord, thank you for hearing and answering our prayers. Help us to acknowledge those answers, even when they don't match our expectations. Amen*

Thought for the day: God always answers my prayers – sometimes in surprising ways.

Max Mardick (Colorado, US)

Guided to serve

Read 2 Corinthians 1:1–7

The God of all comfort… comforts us in all our troubles, so that we can comfort those in any trouble with the comfort we ourselves receive from God.
2 Corinthians 1:3–4 (NIV)

When at the age of 26 I moved to a bustling new city far from my friends and family, I was overcome with loneliness. I began to pray: 'Father, it's miserable being lonely, and I know I'm not the only one. Thank you that I can empathise a little better with people who are far from their families and friends. But what can I do with this situation? Where can I go to make others less lonely?' Nursing homes popped into my mind, so I decided to see if my church had any existing ministries in that area.

But when Sunday came and I scanned a church full of mostly name-less faces, my resolve sank. I'll ask about it next week, I decided, and sat down ready for the service. An elderly woman came and sat beside me. After we exchanged hellos, she told me that she and a group of others had just returned from visiting a nearby nursing home. I learned that they went there every month so I decided to join them. When we sing hymns with the residents, I love to see how much it means to those who take part, and consider it a privilege to be welcomed as their visitor.

In the midst of my loneliness, God brought out a willingness to help others. This led me to recognise the path that he had placed before me – one that took away not only my own loneliness but also some of the lonely feelings of others.

Prayer: *Dear Father, thank you for guiding us in the right paths. Amen*

Thought for the day: While I comfort others, God comforts me.

Christine Duncan (Ontario, Canada)

God's wonderful creation

Read Genesis 1:26–31
God saw all that he had made, and it was very good.
Genesis 1:31 (NIV)

As an artist, I have to focus on details like light, shadow and colour. Often I find inspiration in the beauty of God's creation. Sunsets, mountains and cascading waterfalls have been central to my work – until a few months ago.

Back in January, I began painting faces. What I noticed was just how much harder it is to capture the essence of a person in pencil and acrylics. Get one detail wrong – the nose just a little bit too big or the eyes off centre – and the image is ruined.

After each of the first five days of creation, God looked at what had been created and saw that it was 'good'. On the sixth day of creation, however, after making a human being, God declared that creation was 'very good'. Too often we look around and see the beauty in sunsets, mountains or cascading waterfalls but forget the beauty present in God's greatest, most complex creation – human beings. After all, God loves us enough to send Jesus Christ to live and die so that we can have abundant and eternal life.

Prayer: *Dear God, help us see every human as a unique creation of your love. Amen*

Thought for the day: How do I show love for God's creation?

Nathan Melia (Texas, US)

The greatest witness

Read Romans 10:11–15

Always be prepared to give an answer to everyone who asks you to give the reason for the hope that you have. But do this with gentleness and respect.
1 Peter 3:15 (NIV)

When I became a Christian, I resolved never to miss an opportunity to share my faith with others. One day as my husband and I were admiring our newborn son in the hospital, another patient, Vi, was wheeled into the ward with her newborn girl. I said a prayer for boldness to witness to her.

During the day Vi and I were visited by family and friends, but in the evening after our babies were asleep, we talked about the difficult circumstances of her life. And I listened.

In my conversations with Vi, I learned a lot about witnessing. I know it's important to witness by talking to people about Jesus. However, this experience taught me that listening to the deepest heart-cry of another person is also important. In those times, we may be a link in the chain that eventually connects that person with God.

After three days, Vi and I said goodbye, reluctant to break off our friendship. As my husband prepared to take me and our son home, I thought that I hadn't talked about salvation with Vi. I hadn't prayed with her or shared any Bible verses.

But the Lord reminded me that I had shown love. And that can be the greatest witness of all.

Prayer: *Dear God, help us to take any opportunity we have to share the love of Christ in any way we can. Amen*

Thought for the day: Compassionate listening is one way I can show God's love.

Jewell Johnson (Arizona, US)

Even me

Read Matthew 6:25–33

God so loved the world that he gave his one and only Son, that whoever believes in him shall not perish but have eternal life.
John 3:16 (NIV)

I've always had to work really hard at school. I make many mistakes, and my dad has to point them out and explain them to me. I was so discouraged by my struggles with schoolwork that I began to feel that I didn't deserve any of the good things in my life.

When I expressed my feelings of unworthiness, my dad explained that God may give us challenging tasks but will also help us through them. Dad reminded me of this verse: 'Look at the birds of the air; they do not sow or reap or store away in barns, and yet your heavenly Father feeds them. Are you not much more valuable than they?' (Matthew 6:26). I thought, 'Those birds are so lucky; they don't have to go to school and God still takes care of them!' Then Dad read John 3:16 to remind me how much God loves me.

Even when I get things wrong, God still gives me oxygen, sunshine, food and many good things just because he loves each of us so very much. Now I do my work with more enthusiasm because I know that even when I make mistakes, God is with me and still loves me.

Prayer: *Dear Lord, thank you for caring for us – even when we feel we don't deserve it. In the name of Jesus Christ. Amen*

Thought for the day: I don't have to do anything to earn God's love.

David Serdyukov (Moscow, Russia)

Showing our colours

Read Matthew 13:24–29

The kingdom of heaven is like a man who sowed good seed in his field.
Matthew 13:24 (NIV)

Walking back from shopping yesterday, I passed a garden which has long been neglected and choked with weeds. I hadn't passed this way for a while, so I was delighted to see several large dahlias in flower among the weeds, including an enormous yellow one and another in vibrant red. It was impossible to miss them. The garden was transformed and so was my day!

The experience reminded me that, as Christians, we can be like those dahlias. With God's help we can stand out boldly and flourish in a world where God's word seems neglected and choked by the 'weeds' of the world.

We must try to be bold and show our King's colours. The strife and evil things of the world may gain a foothold for a time, but they will not overcome the truth if we help to declare it. As God's messengers we must not be afraid to be noticed, but people's lives can only be transformed if they know that we are there.

Prayer: *Lord, help us not to be neglectful of your world, but to be bold in living out your gospel. Amen*

Thought for the day: For whom can I be a 'dahlia' today?

Kathleen Sharps (Cheshire, England)

The old coin

Read Psalm 8:3–9

You are no longer a slave but a child, and if a child then also an heir, through God.
Galatians 4:7 (NRSV)

In a junk shop I found an old and somewhat rare coin. Its age and history fascinated me, so I bought it. The value of the coin was stamped on it, but to a collector that coin is worth far more than that. The coin has two values: the value that the government stamped on it and the value that a collector might pay for it.

It seems to me that it is the same way with people. We may feel that society gives us a value based on our social status, income or appearance. But God values us as beloved children for whom Jesus Christ lived, died and was raised again. God is the supreme collector who seeks to gather all of us into the kingdom of compassion, peace and justice. When we accept and treat others as people of intrinsic worth who are endowed with dignity, the kingdom of God draws a bit closer. The lives of others are blessed and, by the grace of God, so are ours.

Prayer: *Help us, Holy One, to see the worth and dignity in everyone we meet, remembering that we are all your beloved children. We pray in the name of Jesus Christ: 'Our Father in heaven, hallowed be your name, your kingdom come, your will be done, on earth as it is in heaven. Give us today our daily bread. Forgive us our debts, as we also have forgiven our debtors. And lead us not into temptation, but deliver us from the evil one.'* Amen*

Thought for the day: I am worth more to God than I can imagine.

Philip Rice (Michigan, US)

PRAYER FOCUS: TO SEE WORTH IN EVERY PERSON
*Matthew 6:9–13 (NIV)

Opportunity in waiting

Read 2 Peter 3:8–11

I watch in hope for the Lord, I wait for God my Saviour; my God will hear me.
Micah 7:7 (NIV)

When we joined the queue for one of my son's favourite attractions at an amusement park, we were told that the waiting time was over an hour and a half. I asked my son if he still wanted to wait, hoping he would opt for something else. He assured me that the attraction was a must, so we began the hot, crowded wait. But we anticipated the thrill of what was to come and before we knew it, we were taking our places on the ride. As soon as it began, the memories of the queue were replaced by the joy of the attraction.

I don't think anyone enjoys waiting. However, scripture reminds us that waiting is part of our life with God. Sometimes the wait seems uncomfortable or unbearable, but God promises to listen when we call out to him. When we spend our time waiting in anticipation of the fulfilment of God's promises, the delay becomes an act of praise.

The long queue at the amusement park gave my son and me an opportunity to connect with each other at a deeper level. Likewise, when we feel that God has not moved according to our preferred time frame, we can explore ways to use that time to grow into a stronger and more trusting relationship with him.

Prayer: *Dear God, help us to find ways to use our times of waiting to grow closer to you. Amen*

Thought for the day: Today I will draw closer to God during times of waiting.

Cortney Whiting (Georgia, US)

PRAYER FOCUS: AMUSEMENT PARK EMPLOYEES

Hope through trials

Read Jeremiah 29:10–14

'I know the plans I have for you,' declares the Lord, 'plans to prosper you and not to harm you, plans to give you hope and a future.'
Jeremiah 29:11 (NIV)

As I was growing up, my family didn't have much money. At one time, four of us had to live in a tiny flat while my mum was finishing her degree. Later, when we moved to a bigger house, we couldn't afford to pay the bills. As a result, our electricity and water would be cut off, and for weeks we'd have to 'live like the pilgrims', as my mum would say. Even through these desperate times, my mother never let us forget that God was with us and watching over us. We would always ask her, 'How can you be so sure? We don't even have water to wash our clothes and there is barely any food in the kitchen!' Then, graciously, she would respond with Jeremiah 29:11.

This verse has carried me through many dark times in my adolescent and young-adult life. I felt assured that if God still had good plans for an exiled people who had continually rejected him, he would be faithful to me as well. Now my mother is working on her doctorate, and our current house overflows with prosperity and love. I have witnessed in my own life that God will never fail us.

Prayer: *Dear God, thank you that your promises are faithful and trustworthy. Amen*

Thought for the day: God never fails me.

Seth Stewart (Texas, US)

Helping hands

Read Mark 10:42–45

The Son of Man did not come to be served, but to serve, and to give his life as a ransom for many.
Mark 10:45 (NIV)

Several years ago I slipped on some ice and landed hard on my hand, badly spraining my wrist. Since I live alone, I had to do everything with one hand for several days. The simplest of tasks, such as buttering a piece of bread, were suddenly difficult. My daughter drove for over an hour just to make me a sandwich and do my washing-up. I soon learned to use my elbows, my knees and even my mouth, along with my one good hand, to cut a sandwich or open an envelope or a packet of biscuits.

I came away from those days of frustration with a new appreciation not only for the gift of my own two hands but also for those who are 'hands' in the body of Christ. I consider those who enjoy lending a hand where it's needed as having the spiritual gift of helping (see 1 Corinthians 12:28).

Thank God for the beautiful hands of those who help with Communion, serve as welcomers, work in the crèche, run errands, help in the office and assist the elderly. I wonder if these Christian servants who care for others have any idea how much their acts of giving mean to those they help.

Prayer: *Dear Lord, use our hands to serve in any way we can, and lift our hearts in gratitude for all those who are serving. Amen*

Thought for the day: My hands are God's gift to serve others.

Ruth Brentner (Illinois, US)

Navigating through life

Read Deuteronomy 11:18–21

Your word is a lamp before my feet and a light for my journey.
Psalm 119:105 (CEB)

During my childhood, whenever my family went on holiday, we children would take turns sitting in the front passenger seat of the car. When it was my turn, my dad would give me the map so I could read it. I loved looking at its squiggly lines and dreaming about where they would take us. I still find paper maps fascinating.

As Christians, the Bible is our map. It guides our lives, gives us direction and reveals God to us. For many years, I wanted to read the Bible to learn more about God, but I didn't know where to start. Then my church provided Bible reading plans, and every year since then I've been using a plan to read through my study Bible. The daily reading gives me a fresh start to each day and something new to discern within God's word.

For many people, printed maps have been replaced by satnavs and smartphone apps, but I'm grateful that the Bible never becomes obsolete. It is an eternal source of wisdom – the map that guides us to our heavenly destination.

Prayer: *Dear God, increase our desire to read your word, seek your guidance and follow you. Amen*

Thought for the day: As we journey through life, God's word is our road map.

Jan Towne (Virginia, US)

One day at a time

Read Hebrews 13:1–6

Do not worry about tomorrow, for tomorrow will worry about itself. Each day has enough trouble of its own.
Matthew 6:34 (NIV)

Recently, I had a minor car accident, my second in less than a year. It made me realise that I was no longer a confident driver due to my macular degeneration. So after 70 years of driving, I gave away my car.

Then I began to imagine all sorts of difficulties that would follow my decision. How will I get to the shops? My doctor's surgery is only about three streets away, but I'm not strong enough to walk that far. I became full of worry and fear about my decision to give up driving.

A few days later, the Lord brought to my mind ways I could cope with this new life. I thought of my friends, who had often offered to give me a lift. I thought of the services in our town for people like me – minibuses taking people to the shops and volunteer car drivers for health appointments. I could occasionally take a taxi, using the money I had saved from giving up my car. God seemed to be telling me not to worry, that help would come as each challenge arose.

Don't be anxious about the rest of your life, Jesus tells us. Deal only with today. Each day has its own troubles, so don't take on the troubles that might possibly come up in the future.

Now, though I still have problems getting to some places, I am no longer afraid. I know that God and my friends are there to see me through.

Prayer: *Dear God, you help us in countless ways. Continue to remind us that you are with us, even in the major changes of our lives. Amen*

Thought for the day: God knows my needs and in time will provide.

Ken Claar (Idaho, US)

Blurred vision

Read Colossians 3:12–17

Be devoted to one another in love. Honour one another above yourselves.
Romans 12:10 (NIV)

Most mornings as I put my contact lenses in, I pray, 'Thank you, God, for the gift of sight.' But one morning after a difficult evening at church with the youth group, I used the time instead for a moaning session. 'I've had enough, God. I've finished volunteering with young people. They're not appreciative. They're disrespectful. They're just a crowd of self-absorbed kids who can't focus for even one minute on anything but themselves.' All the time I was struggling with my contact lenses. I fumbled with one and dropped the other. Aloud, I half-heartedly asked God, 'What are you trying to tell me – that I'm seeing this all wrong?'

With some thought, I realised that I had been the self-absorbed one. Instead of seeing the young person with recently separated parents, I saw bad behaviour. Instead of seeing someone with an underage drinking problem, I saw disrespect. Where I should have seen someone struggling with a self-harm problem, I saw anger. God reminded me that Jesus 'took the children in his arms' (Mark 10:16). He loved them, cared for them and was deeply concerned about their lives. And we are called to show the same compassion.

So I prayed – for the young people, for their issues and for my blurred vision. And I vowed that rather than showing them my disapproval, I would show them my love. I think God just might want us to relate to everyone this way.

Prayer: *Dear God, help us to love your children as Jesus does – with arms wide open and hands ready to bless. Amen*

Thought for the day: Every day, I will try to see others the way God sees them.

Julie Lavender (Georgia, US)

Joy always

Read Romans 5:3–5

Rejoice always, pray continually, give thanks in all circumstances; for this is God's will for you in Christ Jesus.
1 Thessalonians 5:16–18 (NIV)

My wife and I are retired and take care of our two young grandsons while our daughter and her husband are at work. Because we love our grandsons, we hate to see them crying or in distress. When they are ill or hungry, we joyfully supply what they need.

If we, as imperfect human beings, hate to see our children unhappy, why should we be surprised that God might feel the same? But the sacrifice of God's only Son, Jesus Christ, far surpasses whatever we might have to endure. And Jesus also had to be willing to sacrifice himself on the cross and shed his blood for the salvation of the whole world. God and Jesus want us to have eternal life, to someday be free from all kinds of pain. In the meantime, Paul encourages us to rejoice and even give thanks when we face times that call us to sacrifice: 'Rejoice always… give thanks in all circumstances.' These words assure us that our faithful obedience will bring us 'wisdom, knowledge and joy' (Ecclesiastes 2:26, CEB).

Prayer: *Holy God, give us strength to remain joyous in all circumstances, so that you may be glorified. Amen*

Thought for the day: Like a good parent, God joyfully supplies what I need.

Stanley Solanki (Maharashtra, India)

Strength in Christ

Read Philippians 4:10–13

My flesh and my heart may fail, but God is the strength of my heart and my portion forever.
Psalm 73:26 (NRSV)

I am the oldest of seven children. During my last year at college, my family had only one car, so I would have to get up very early every morning and take my mum to work. After that I would come home to make breakfast for my younger brothers and sisters and see that they all got to school or to the childminder. After doing all that, I would finally get myself ready for school.

Some days I felt too tired to complete all these responsibilities, but I tried never to complain. After one very hectic morning, I was simply overwhelmed. That's when I remembered the scripture, 'I can do all things through [Christ] who strengthens me' (Philippians 4:13). I knew that I had to pray – to ask Christ for strength to continue.

Everyone has certain responsibilities, and sometimes they become draining. In a world where everything moves so fast, we can easily feel overwhelmed. How important it is, then, to slow down and ask God to give us the strength to continue in the work that each day brings us.

Prayer: *Heavenly Father, give us the strength we need each day to continue in our work, always aware of your purpose for our lives. Amen*

Thought for the day: What may seem impossible for me is possible through Christ.

Gozeila Bilal (South Dakota, US)

A long way from home

Read Genesis 28:10–22

The Lord will guide you continually, and satisfy your needs in parched places, and make your bones strong.
Isaiah 58:11 (NRSV)

I was 31 years old and at a major crossroads in my life. For the previous four years I had been teaching on an island in the South Pacific, and my contract was coming to an end. My house was isolated from the village. I had no telephone and no church family. I was newly divorced and soon to be unemployed. Although I was thousands of miles from home, I felt close to God there.

As I thought about my uncertain future, I walked up the dirt road with the blue sky overhead and sunshine on my face. I asked God for direction: 'Should I go back to live with my parents in the United States? Should I return to college? Should I look for another job overseas? What should I do?'

The answer came soundlessly but clearly: 'Do as you choose. Just remember that I am with you, and whatever you do, do it with me.' Peace and reassurance flowed into me. I would find a direction for my future, and I would be fine.

Forty years have passed since that day. It is just as God said to Jacob, 'I am with you and will watch over you wherever you go' (Genesis 28:15, NIV). As I look back, I see God's loving presence in every step of my life's journey.

Prayer: *Dear God, it is a great comfort to know that you are with us and will never leave us. Thank you for your faithfulness to us. Amen*

Thought for the day: Whatever I do, God will be by my side.

Karen Lewis (Florida, US)

True gratitude

Read 1 Timothy 6:6–16

If we have food and clothing, we will be content with that.
1 Timothy 6:8 (NIV)

Recently I listened to a sermon about how we show gratitude by wanting what we have, not by getting what we want. As an inmate on death row, I am very restricted about what I can do and have, so I am constantly asking God for more. Recently, however, I have been praying to God to help me be more grateful for what I already have, instead of fixating on what I lack.

Yesterday, I prepared soup in the prison kitchen. While it cooked, I worked on finishing a writing project. As I smelled the soup's delicious aroma, my stomach rumbled in anticipation. I was thankful that I had the soup to satisfy my hunger. At that moment joy flooded my soul, and I prayed, 'Lord, thank you for the soup and for answering my prayer for gratitude.' I could sense God's pleasure that I appreciated the gifts that I had been given. I then realised that God had given me all I need and always would. And I was content.

Prayer: *Dear God, help us always to appreciate what you have given us. Amen*

Thought for the day: Gratitude to God helps fuel contentment.

George T. Wilkerson (North Carolina, US)

Pushing past obstacles

Read Judges 7:1–8; 8:11–12

[Jesus said,] 'If you have faith and do not doubt… you can say to this mountain, "Go, throw yourself into the sea," and it will be done.'
Matthew 21:21 (NIV)

My husband, Kamlesh, had a dream of completing his college degree while working full-time. During his third year of study, his examinations were moved forward by two months. My husband was worried since he had a lot less time to prepare. I encouraged him with God's words to Gideon in today's reading: 'With the three hundred men… I will save you and give the Midianites into your hands' (v. 7). I told Kamlesh that if God could give Gideon the victory even when his forces had dropped from 22,000 men to only 300, then God could also give him success even though he had fewer days to study. God did indeed bless Kamlesh so that he passed his exams.

In God's plan, Gideon was not to receive success through thousands of warriors, because then the people would think that they had won the battle through their strength alone. So God gave them victory with only 300 soldiers. In a similar way, God gave my husband success, despite obstacles such as difficult courses, less time to study and many responsibilities with his job and family. At first these obstacles piled up to become what seemed to be an unscalable mountain; but as we trusted God's word, he helped us to arrive at the top. And we give the glory to him.

Prayer: *Dear God, thank you for helping us to persevere to reach our goals even through many trials and difficulties. In Jesus' name. Amen*

Thought for the day: Even through obstacles, God gives us victory.

Sushma Kamlesh Macwan (Gujarat, India)

Finding kindness

Read Galatians 5:16–25

The fruit of the Spirit is love, joy, peace, patience, kindness, generosity, faithfulness, gentleness, and self-control.
Galatians 5:22–23 (NRSV)

On one of those days when there was too much to do and too little time to do it, I rushed to a fast-food outlet and was greeted by an angry, 'What do you want?' After placing my order, I realised that God was giving me an opportunity to grow. I gave the woman a half-smile and asked, 'Bad day?' Then came a flood of all the things that had gone wrong – fryer broken, workers not turning up, problems with deliveries. I said something like, 'That really is a bad day! I hope things get better. God bless.'

As I left, I glanced back to see a smile on the worker's face. All it had taken to help make her day a little better was for a stranger to show some kindness. I've never forgotten that encounter because it was a moment when I felt that I was in step with the Spirit, living according to the example Jesus set for us.

Today's reading describes qualities that Jesus modelled for us and challenges us to aspire to be more like Christ. When we pray to grow more Christlike in our actions, the Lord will give us opportunities to show just how we have grown – often in the most ordinary places.

Prayer: *Lord Jesus, fill us with the fruit of your Spirit. Help us to seek opportunities to model each one. Amen*

Thought for the day: Today I will look for ways to show the fruit of the Spirit to those around me.

Dave Caswell (Arkansas, US)

Becoming known

Read 1 John 1:1–4

As iron sharpens iron, so one person sharpens another.
Proverbs 27:17 (NIV)

For a few years, I have been attending a weekly Bible study house group that expands my understanding of scripture. We also share a delicious meal. Many of us didn't know one another well until the leader began asking people to describe how they came to claim Jesus as their Saviour. We heard stories of faith found, then abandoned, then reclaimed. We learned of the role of family in finding faith and listened in awe to descriptions of events that only God could orchestrate.

In some ways, our Bible study group resembles the early Christian house churches described in Acts 2:42. We share a meal, learn from scripture and, as we tell our stories, I imagine that we experience enthusiasm similar to that of the apostles and other followers as they talked about their personal encounters with Jesus and the world-changing events unfolding around them.

It is wonderful to experience Christians relating to each other as spiritual brothers and sisters, mothers and fathers, sons and daughters. A small group is the perfect setting for these relationships to form and grow as we open up our lives to others. When Christians take this opportunity, we honour God. And when we experience the support, wisdom and unconditional love that are hallmarks of a spiritual family, we have even more reason to worship God and to trust in the promises in the Bible.

Prayer: *Dear God, help us to share our personal stories as we form bonds of faith that are not easily broken. Amen*

Thought for the day: 'How good… it is when God's people live together in unity!' (Psalm 133:1).

Kenneth Avon White (North Carolina, US)

Honest with God

Read Romans 8:31–39

Nothing can separate us from God's love in Christ Jesus our Lord: not death or life, not angels or rulers, not present things or future things, not powers or height or depth, or any other thing that is created.
Romans 8:38–39 (CEB)

I never really understood this verse until a few years ago when I was faced with the death of my oldest child. I went through many conflicting emotions and they left me feeling confused. I was brought up to believe that I should never be angry about anything that God allowed to happen. However, when I read this verse again, God reminded me that I am human and he is God.

Nothing. That word really spoke to me. 'Really, God? Nothing will separate us from you?' God assured me of this scriptural truth, but I realised that this passage does not say that nothing bad will ever happen. It says that nothing can separate us from God – not even the tragic and untimely death of a loved one.

When we realise that God is always with us, we can lay our true feelings at his feet. Then we can begin to heal in the ways God has promised. And that healing brings us peace.

Prayer: *Dear Lord, help us to realise that you are God and that we can bring our hurts to you, knowing that you care for us and hear our cries for help. Amen*

Thought for the day: Even when I am angry, God is with me.

Jennifer Floyd (Florida, US)

Who is my neighbour?

Read Luke 10:25–37

Dear children, let us not love with words or speech but with actions and in truth.
1 John 3:18 (NIV)

When I was driving slowly out of a small shopping-centre car park, a frantic young woman rapped on my car window. She pleaded, 'Could you help me? I've recently moved here and came for a job interview this morning. Now my car won't start, and I don't know what to do. I'm staying with my brother and have been trying to phone him, but he's not answering.' I asked where her brother lived and she replied, 'It's about 20 minutes away. But I don't have any money to pay for a taxi.'

I had an appointment of my own, but I felt that I couldn't leave her stranded. I offered to give her money for a taxi. She dabbed her eyes and accepted gratefully.

While driving away I prayed for that young woman and remembered Jesus' parable of the good Samaritan. The scribe's question was, 'Who is my neighbour?' Most of us think of our neighbours as the people who live next door. According to Jesus, our neighbour is anyone we meet who is in need and whom we can help, no matter how dissimilar we are. As we show kindness to those in need, we demonstrate our love for God.

Prayer: *Gracious God, open our eyes and our hearts to our neighbours in need. May each act of kindness be an expression of our love for you. Amen*

Thought for the day: I express my love for God when I show kindness to my neighbours.

Geraldine Nicholas (Alberta, Canada)

Investing

Read Micah 6:6–8

What does the Lord require of you? To act justly and to love mercy and to walk humbly with your God.
Micah 6:8 (NIV)

During my career, I invested in a retirement savings plan. I set aside some of our finances for long-term growth so that my wife and I would have enough money to sustain us for the rest of our lives. Before I retired, I had thought about investing only in the context of money. But afterwards, I started asking myself, 'How can I invest in my Christianity and in leading a life of faith?'

Now I daily set aside time for devotional reading and prayer. Also, I try always to act justly and to love others. I believe that investing my actions in this way will help to sustain my relationship with God and my service to others.

Only God can evaluate our actions and judge the return on our investment. If we want to be like Christ, then we will invest in ways that serve others.

Prayer: *Dear God, thank you for your presence in our lives. Give us the strength to do justice, love others and walk humbly with you. As Jesus taught us, we pray, 'Father, hallowed be your name, your kingdom come. Give us each day our daily bread. Forgive us our sins, for we also forgive everyone who sins against us. And lead us not into temptation.'* Amen*

Thought for the day: What will I do today to invest in my relationship with God?

Mike Wilt (West Virginia, US)

PRAYER FOCUS: FINANCIAL PLANNERS
*Luke 11:2–4

Productive pruning

Read John 15:1–8

[God] cuts off every branch in me that bears no fruit, while every branch that does bear fruit he prunes so that it will be even more fruitful.

John 15:2 (NIV)

Every year I had searched beneath the prickly briars of my raspberry bushes for ripe berries with no success. Then I read an article about how to increase my yield. The writer pointed out that raspberries produce fruit on new growth. The article explained how to cut away old branches to expose new shoots to more sunlight, allow access to more nutrients from the soil and provide extra space for growth. Heeding the advice, I pruned the old stems. When I had finished, I felt sure that the severe cutting would ruin the plants, so imagine my surprise the following spring when my bushes rewarded me with an abundant harvest!

In John's gospel, Jesus refers to God as the gardener who cuts off every branch that fails to bear fruit. He also prunes fruitful branches to produce greater yields. I considered how my spiritual life needed pruning. For example, simply repeating the same actions or words may stifle effective witnessing or hinder prayer life. Bible reading without meditating or seeking God's guidance may become meaningless. Busyness may replace more urgent Christian service.

God prunes us in different ways to refocus us on our faith. When he lops off old habits and refreshes our commitment to prayer, Bible study and service, we produce more abundant fruit for the kingdom.

Prayer: *Father God, thank you for seasons of pruning that result in greater harvests of fruit for you. Amen*

Thought for the day: God's pruning helps me to produce more fruit for the kingdom.

Linda Ross Shoaf (Mississippi, US)

An unexpected hour

Read Luke 10:38–42

Be still, and know that I am God!
Psalm 46:10 (NRSV)

I anticipated a hectic day at work, juggling meetings and projects with deadlines. Even lunchtime was set aside for a working meeting. I decided to jot down a plan, listing which tasks I would tackle in which hour. I could get everything done if I stuck to my agenda, but I had no time to spare.

At 11 o'clock, I was relieved that everything I needed to finish before my two-hour lunch meeting was complete. As I waited for others to arrive for the meeting, I realised that I had made a mistake. My lunch meeting did not actually begin until noon, and it was set for one hour, not two. The extra, unplanned hour was a gift. I considered using the time to continue working. Instead, I sat down and planted my feet on the ground. With one hand on my chest and the other on my stomach, I felt the rise and fall of each breath. I made each breath deeper, slower. With each inhale, I asked God to refresh and still my soul.

As I took advantage of the unexpected pause in my day, I recalled the words Jesus spoke to Martha, whose name I share: 'Martha, Martha, you are worried and distracted by many things; there is need of only one thing' (Luke 10:41–42). I was reminded that, even on the busiest of days, I can make room for God in my schedule.

Prayer: *Creator God, help us to balance the mundane tasks of our day and those things of lasting importance. Create in us clean hearts and renewed spirits. Amen*

Thought for the day: When I set aside a time to rest with God, I can better serve the rest of the day.

Marti Williams-Martin (Tennessee, US)

Hiding in plain sight

Read Galatians 6:1–10
Each one should test their own actions. Then they can take pride in themselves alone, without comparing themselves to someone else.
Galatians 6:4 (NIV)

While working in a large chain store, I soon noticed something about one of the customers. He was in the shop several times a day, walking around talking to people, but rarely did he buy anything. As the months went by, I would see him outside sitting in his vehicle for hours at a time with lots of clothes stored in the back. I thought that he didn't look homeless and I spoke to him a couple of times. He told me of his many college degrees and his employment history. At the moment he was unemployed.

One day I felt a strong urge to approach the man and offer help. Like many Christians, the fear of offending him entered my mind. I said a quick prayer for guidance and offered to help him. He refused the help, but I felt glad I had tried.

Stepping out of our comfort zone is not easy, but Jesus teaches us to help those in need. When God calls us to lend a hand to someone, it may not be in the most comfortable situation, and we risk being rejected. But isn't the risk worth it?

Prayer: *Heavenly Father, help us to pour out your love to people in need, knowing that our small acts of kindness may change the course of someone's day. In Jesus' name, we pray. Amen*

Thought for the day: Today I will offer help to those whom God has placed in my path.

Joshua D. Berrier (North Carolina, US)

Turning around

Read Jonah 1:1–3; 3:1–10

When God saw what [the Ninevites] did and how they turned from their evil ways, he relented and did not bring on them the destruction he had threatened.
Jonah 3:10 (NIV)

I used to think that the wrong turns in my life were irreversible. When I was growing up, I wasn't allowed to change my initial decisions, and I thought that God dealt with us the same way. But scripture reveals that God not only allows second chances but also urges us to correct our unwise choices, even if it takes some time.

When Jonah received his assignment from God, he ran in the opposite direction and ended up inside a great fish (see Jonah 1:3, 17). Even after he repented, he could not proclaim God's message immediately. First he had to escape from the fish, and then he had to travel a long distance to Nineveh. But when he cried out for God's help, he received it, and helped save an entire city from destruction.

Whenever we need to change direction, God stands ready to help us. If we encounter hindrances in turning around, all we need to do is ask for divine assistance. It is never too late to say yes to the Lord's commands.

Prayer: *Forgiving God, help us to overcome any obstacles that prevent us from heading in the right direction. Amen*

Thought for the day: When I need to change direction, God is there to help.

Diana Savage (Washington, US)

Sanctuary

Read Psalm 31:19–22
You have been a refuge for the poor, a refuge for the needy in their distress, a shelter from the storm and a shade from the heat.
Isaiah 25:4 (NIV)

A violent hailstorm ripped through many parts of my city. Our church windows were not spared when the golf-ball-sized hailstones punched through them. On Sunday morning, as I sat in a quiet space in a room with broken windows, I wondered what good could come from this damage.

Later, I was delighted to find that pigeons had found refuge from the storm in the holes in the windows. Their cooing brought the sound of real peace to a place where we pray for peace every Sunday. This brought to mind the vital role many churches played during the 1980s in the struggle to end apartheid. Places of worship became sanctuaries for those being hounded by the police. The house of God is a sanctuary – a place of healing and recovery for those who hurt, for those in need, for those who seek shelter from the storm.

Somehow out of the bad comes good. It depends on how we choose to view the storms of life. Yes, hail does bring damage, but it can also open new ways in which pigeons – and all of us – can find sanctuary in God's house.

Prayer: *Loving God, we pray for those who seek shelter from the storms of life. Amen*

Thought for the day: How can I help make my church a true sanctuary?

Roland Rink (Gauteng, South Africa)

A way out

Read 1 Corinthians 10:8–13
God is faithful; he will not let you be tempted beyond what you can bear. But when you are tempted, he will also provide a way out so that you can endure it.
1 Corinthians 10:13 (NIV)

Anxious to get home after a long day at work, I rushed through my shopping and did not notice that the cashier had accidentally given me too much change. As I neared the exit, I realised the mistake, and thoughts started streaming in my mind: 'Walk faster. No one will know.' Then another thought followed: 'This must be a test.'

This last thought played on my mind because this was the second such experience I'd had that day. Earlier, I had accidentally almost left a public bus without paying for the fare; but then I felt God telling me that if I continued on my way and didn't pay, I would be committing a sin. If instead I went back to pay, I would be growing and maturing for the glory of God. I paid my bus fare and gave back the extra change to the supermarket assistant as well.

Being short of money and yet having two challenges involving money in one day reminded me of the way temptations sometimes storm our lives and cloud our judgement, to the extent that we start viewing things that are wrong as right. But God is faithful and knows us; he never stops giving us instruction and the help we need to endure temptation.

Prayer: *Mighty God, thank you for delivering us from temptations today. In Jesus' name. Amen*

Thought for the day: Today, with every temptation, I will look to God for the way out.

Vimbai Chizarura (Mashonaland East, Zimbabwe)

Invisible barriers

Read Hebrews 12:1–3

The heart is deceitful above all things and beyond cure. Who can understand it?
Jeremiah 17:9 (NIV)

A bee entered the passenger-side window of my car and headed straight for the clear windscreen, trying to escape. For several minutes it bumped against the glass. When the bee approached my side of the car, I opened my door and it flew out to freedom.

As I thought of the bee's actions, I wondered how many invisible barriers in my life keep me from experiencing the full freedom and blessings that God wants me to enjoy. Are there buried resentments, hidden pride, fears, stale traditions, false beliefs or passive rebellion that I haven't noticed?

Jeremiah 17:9 tells us that, though we think we understand our hearts and minds, we can never fully understand ourselves or our motives. Jeremiah went on to record, 'I the Lord search the heart and examine the mind' (17:10). Because only God can fully understand us, we can pray along with David: 'Search me, God, and know my heart; test me and know my anxious thoughts. See if there is any offensive way in me, and lead me in the way everlasting' (Psalm 139:23–24). We can rely on God to help us recognise the invisible barriers that are keeping us from Christ's freedom and blessings.

Prayer: *Dear Lord, reveal to us the hidden areas of our lives that prevent us from finding full freedom in Christ. Amen*

Thought for the day: God can help me discover the invisible barriers that keep me from being free in Christ.

Steven Thompson (Iowa, US)

God's salvation

Read Ephesians 2:1–10

By grace you have been saved through faith, and this is not your own doing; it is the gift of God.
Ephesians 2:8 (NRSV)

I live in a city where students are very competitive. I got used to competition at a young age and became focused on staying at the top. Whenever a classmate performed better than I did, I would tell myself that I would do better than them next time. But even when I did, instead of feeling happy I felt filled with overwhelming pressure and fatigue.

Following my second year at university, I developed serious flu-like symptoms, and I started losing weight. I managed to finish my final year of university, but I was apprehensive about my future. I wondered what I could possibly do after graduation when I was in such a poor physical condition.

Scripture offered me great comfort during that time, and it continues to help me today. The Bible reminds me that we are saved by the grace of God. Our salvation is a gift. God does not require top grades, a certain status or huge success. Loving grace is readily given to anyone who reaches out to God. Even during difficult periods, he continually restores us through scripture and love.

Prayer: *Gracious God, thank you that our salvation does not depend on our achievements. Help us to feel your presence in all the different times of our lives. Amen*

Thought for the day: God loves me regardless of my achievements.

Flo Au (Hong Kong, China)

PRAYER FOCUS: THOSE WHO FEEL THEIR WORTH DEPENDS ON THEIR ACHIEVEMENTS

God, our shepherd

Read Psalm 55:1–8

Cast your cares on the Lord and he will sustain you.
Psalm 55:22 (NIV)

The doctor told my sister and me that our dear mother only had months to live due to congestive heart failure. I went home to collect some personal items for Mum before returning to the hospital. When I got into the house, I dropped the keys on the floor, slumped into a chair and began sobbing. My best friend, the person who began my life, would shortly be gone. I felt helpless and alone. I didn't know where to turn and didn't have anyone to guide me. What's more, I knew that my family would turn to me for support. All I could do was pray: 'Oh, God, I don't know how to do this, and I don't know to whom or where to turn.'

Still in tears, I returned to the hospital. The hospital's staff and support personnel cared for me from that moment through the last five months of my mother's life. During that time, I wanted for nothing; I experienced a peace that passed all understanding. When we are troubled, we can turn our situation over to God through prayer.

Prayer: *Dear God, forgive us when we forget that you are ever-present in our lives. Help us to remember that even through difficult times, you care for us unconditionally. Amen*

Thought for the day: I can bring anything to God in prayer.

John W. Brigman (Alabama, US)

Squeezing out forgiveness

Read Matthew 18:21–35

Get rid of all bitterness, rage and anger, brawling and slander, along with every form of malice. Be kind and compassionate to one another, forgiving each other, just as in Christ God forgave you.
Ephesians 4:31–32 (NIV)

Recently, I saw an old friend who had hurt me deeply. We smiled at each other and briefly spoke. But inside I still felt bitter. Since the betrayal had happened years ago, I thought I'd forgiven her, but obviously I had not. And once again, the anger and pain felt fresh and overwhelming.

Then I felt the Holy Spirit bring today's scripture to my mind. And I recalled the purple sponge in my kitchen sink. You see, the sponge can't absorb bitter coffee and squeeze out sweet apple juice. So why do I believe I can hold on to bitterness and pour out compassion and forgiveness? As with the sponge, what I soak up is what will come out.

Today's verse reminds us to 'get rid of bitterness… and… every form of malice', then encourages us to 'be kind and compassionate… forgiving each other', just as God forgives us. Only when we make room for kindness, compassion and forgiveness can we get rid of bitterness and malice. If Christ can forgive me, then surely I can forgive my friend. Today I'm going to begin by trusting God to empty out my bitterness as I pray regularly for my friend.

Prayer: *Dear Father, thank you for loving and forgiving us. Help us to release bitterness and malice so that we may be filled with kindness and compassion. In Jesus' name. Amen*

Thought for the day: I can show Christlike compassion by forgiving others.

Tammy C. Van Gils (Virginia, US)

God is always with us

Read Psalm 25:1–7

The Lord your God goes with you; he will never leave you nor forsake you.
Deuteronomy 31:6 (NIV)

In December 2009, I was diagnosed with nasopharynx cancer, commonly known as nose cancer, and began my two-month-long treatment. God's words in Matthew 6:25 came to my wife almost instantly: 'Do not worry.' She immediately prayed to God asking for help. More than seven years later, I am still free from cancer.

Before my illness my wife and I had not attended church for many years. We were living in our own way and going astray. We had no real purpose in life apart from working and taking care of the family. That scary medical diagnosis brought me and my family back to church.

Ministers and brothers and sisters in Christ prayed for us. We have become part of the church family and the body of Christ, and we have become closer to God. We thank him for the love, grace, mercy and faithfulness shown towards our family. God has always kept the promise never to leave or forsake us. When I was wandering like a lost sheep, he found me and brought me back. No matter where we are or what we go through, he is with us. Praise God!

Prayer: *Gracious God, thank you for your love and for always taking care of us. Bring us closer to you and keep us with you. Amen*

Thought for the day: In good times and in bad, God shows me love through the care of others.

Kong Peng Sun (Singapore)

Helping others

Read Matthew 25:31–46

Do not judge, and you will not be judged. Do not condemn, and you will not be condemned. Forgive, and you will be forgiven. Give, and it will be given to you.
Luke 6:37–38 (NIV)

We were at the train station with our son, working out his route to university. The information boards were large and confusing. A young lad asked us if he could help, and when I said yes, he very politely informed us which train my son needed, the platform it would go from and when the next train would arrive.

We thanked him for his help, and then he said, 'Can I ask a favour?' He said that when he had tried to buy his own ticket, his bank card would not work in the machine and he was worried about getting home. So I bought the ticket for him. He thanked us and rushed off to get his train. My son said, 'Do you think he was conning you, Dad?' I said that if he were ever in trouble, I would like to think someone would help him out.

Three days later our son returned to his parked car only to find that his own bank card would not work in the paying machine. With a queue building up behind him, a gentleman tapped him on the shoulder and offered to pay his parking fee. He didn't ask for the money back, but was content to help my son in a tricky situation.

I pray every day that the Lord will watch over my children, and I know he certainly was that day, just as he was watching over the other young man we had helped at the train station.

Prayer: *Lord, thank you for bringing us together so that we can support each other in difficult situations. Amen*

Thought for the day: When I get the opportunity to help someone, I will!

Kevin Boulton (Cheshire, England)

In God's hands

Read Psalm 31:9–16

My times are in your hands.
Psalm 31:15 (NIV)

I used to feel pressured by time constraints and would drive hurriedly, trying to beat traffic lights or pass other drivers. One day when things weren't going my way and everything seemed to frustrate my attempts to save time, a thought came to me: 'Your time is in God's hands.' I relaxed and drove more slowly and considerately. Surprisingly, I arrived on time.

I have seen proof of my time being in God's hands in other ways as well. When I give my time to God in the morning by worshipping through meditations like those in *The Upper Room*, I find that God seems to stretch my time, and I get things done more easily and with less effort than on the days when I don't worship this way. Our time is truly in God's hands.

Prayer: *God of all times and places, receive our praise and gratitude as we see your work in our lives. We pray as Jesus taught us, saying, 'Our Father which art in heaven, Hallowed be thy name. Thy kingdom come, Thy will be done in earth, as it is in heaven. Give us this day our daily bread. And forgive us our debts, as we forgive our debtors. And lead us not into temptation, but deliver us from evil: For thine is the kingdom, and the power, and the glory, forever. Amen.'**

Thought for the day: Today I will trust God with my time.

Carol S. Marti (Galicia, Spain)

Wearing our badge

Read John 18:25–27

Jesus said to his disciples, 'Whoever wants to be my disciple must deny themselves and take up their cross and follow me.'
Matthew 16:24 (NIV)

I am both a police officer and police chaplain and wear a different badge for each role. Just as my head can accommodate only one hat at a time, my uniform can accommodate only one badge. Because the role of chaplain is an on-call position, sometimes I decline requests when they conflict with my main job as a police officer. Sometimes I say no to requests because I don't like getting up in front of hundreds of people and giving the closing blessing. I don't always feel like putting on the chaplain badge.

I have always struggled with wearing my Christian badge of faith as well. It was partly this struggle that motivated me to become a police chaplain because I thought that this role would make it impossible to hide my faith. And yet, although I have stepped up to fulfil countless chaplain duties, I can still deny that call.

Each believer has a badge of faith to wear, and Jesus encourages us to pin it on every morning and let it shine all day long through our words and deeds. However, we may back away from publicly living out our faith for fear of ridicule, rejection or even persecution. And those times when we choose to hide our badge, we know that our merciful Lord is waiting to shine it back up, pin it back on and send us back into the world to serve him.

Prayer: *Dear Lord Jesus, restore us when we back away from declaring our faith. Give us strength to let it shine again. Amen*

Thought for the day: Every day I am called to reflect my faith through my words and actions.

Stephen Johnson (California, US)

Ashes

Read Genesis 33:1–10

[Jacob said to Esau,] 'To see your face is like seeing the face of God, now that you have received me favourably.'
Genesis 33:10 (NIV)

For a long time my brother and I didn't get on. As a child, I idolised him and followed him everywhere – but he didn't want me there. He seemed to delight in making me cry or making me angry. Even as adults, we couldn't be in the same room together without quarrelling. I longed to be friends with him, but my anger – left over from childhood – got in the way.

One day when I was praying, I realised that my brother didn't know that I still hurt from the distant past, so I should stop waiting for him to apologise to me. I knew from my Bible reading that God wanted me to forgive my brother. But I wondered how I could forgive him and also let him know I had forgiven him without making him feel bad, too.

I wrote down all his past actions that still made me angry. After I had read each action, I stopped and asked God to help me forgive my brother and be released from anger. Then, I burned the paper and sent my brother the ashes. In a note, I told him I no longer held anything against him. Although he never mentioned the note to me, our relationship changed. I have changed, too. It didn't happen overnight, but I am free from anger and we are now friends.

Prayer: *Forgiving God, thank you for teaching us to forgive so that we can be free to love you and each other. Amen*

Thought for the day: I can repair a relationship by forgiving someone as God forgives me.

Jane Reid (Oregon, US)

Keep sowing seeds

Read 1 Thessalonians 1

We are God's handiwork, created in Christ Jesus to do good works,
which God prepared in advance for us to do.
Ephesians 2:10 (NIV)

Last week a friend came to thank me for teaching his son English for free. The boy's father said he had nothing with which to repay my kindness – only thanks and a longing to help me if I needed it. He told me that I had also encouraged him to help others without expecting any reward.

Whatever our current employment and ministry, the Bible invites us to continue to do our best in the work that God entrusts to us. Maybe others consider our work trivial. We may see it as a small job that produces little, and we may not often see the fruits of our work.

The good that we share in the world as followers of Christ has no doubt produced much fruit – even if we are unaware of it. One good deed that we do sincerely today can have an impact later on. Therefore, if we continue to sow the seeds of God's goodness, he will grow them and – in time – they will bear fruit in the lives of his people.

Prayer: *Dear God, help us to offer sincere and loving kindness to the people we meet today. Amen*

Thought for the day: One act of love today can have a powerful impact – today or tomorrow.

Linda Chandra (Banten, Indonesia)

Passing it on

Read 2 Timothy 3:10–17

God's righteousness reaches to the grandchildren of those who keep his covenant and remember to keep his commands.
Psalm 103:17–18 (CEB)

Our daughter is pregnant with our seventh grandchild. At a recent baby shower, as gifts for the baby were opened, I reflected on how much this child is already loved. But I also realised that as mother and grandmother, my daughter and I will each have an influential role to play in the life of this little boy.

Paul's letter to Timothy credits his grandmother Lois and his mother Eunice with teaching Timothy the scriptures that brought him to faith. Paul challenged Timothy to continue in what he had been taught from childhood. He had learned from the best; Lois and Eunice were excellent role models in showing how to continue in faithful living.

Like Lois and Eunice, we all have a role to play in teaching the truths of God to the children in our lives. When we are intentional in passing on our faith to the next generation, then they, in turn, can teach their children.

Prayer: *Father God, help us to continue in the truth we have been taught. Amen*

Thought for the day: For whom will I be a role model of faith today?

Glenda Moore (Illinois, US)

No limits

Read Matthew 8:14–17

[Jesus said,] 'Ask and it will be given to you; seek and you will find; knock and the door will be opened to you.'
Matthew 7:7 (NIV)

When my mother became debilitated with dementia, she came to live with me. Her doctor prescribed medication, but she continued to decline. Her behaviour became increasingly hostile and eventually she failed to recognise her family. I became exhausted and discouraged.

My constant prayer had been for strength and grace to care for Mum or, if that failed, wisdom in placing her in a nursing home. But one night I read about how Jesus healed Peter's mother-in-law. It had not occurred to me to ask God to heal my mum. After all, wasn't this disease too hard to heal? Then I remembered that the Lord is not limited by any human problem. I gladly invited Christ to heal my mother.

There was no immediate change. We continued with daily routines and challenges, but gradually Mum became more co-operative, began to recall relationships and was more at peace. When my cousin remarked on her mental clarity, I knew my prayer had been answered. Mum lived for two more years, praying faithfully for her family members by name.

Whether my mother was misdiagnosed, stabilised by medication, helped by routine or miraculously healed is irrelevant to me. One thing I know: I asked and God answered.

Prayer: *Dear Lord Jesus, thank you for your compassion and help. Give us the courage to ask you for what we need and want, not just what we think is possible. Amen*

Thought for the day: There are no limitations on what God can do.

Sharon Beaty (Alabama, US)

Return for deposit

Read 2 Corinthians 1:21–22

[God] put his Spirit in our hearts as a deposit, guaranteeing what is to come.
2 Corinthians 1:22 (NIV)

During the school summer holidays, I often spent time with my grandparents. One of my favourite memories is of having cold soft drinks from their fridge. At home, we had plastic two-litre bottles, but my grandparents had the old-fashioned glass bottles. Having grown up at a time when almost everything was disposable, I usually just threw the empty bottles away. Once, my grandmother fished the bottle out of the bin and pointed to the label that said 'Return for Deposit'. She explained that when she bought soft drinks in glass bottles, she had to pay a little extra; but when she returned the bottles, the shop would return her deposit. That kept the bottles from ending up in landfill and also saved the drinks company money.

In a time when people as well as things seem disposable, it is good to remember the words of 2 Corinthians 1:22. Paul tells us that God has placed a deposit in our hearts. That deposit is the Holy Spirit – a guarantee of the good things to come. God will not toss us aside or forget us. No matter how empty we might become, God's Spirit fills us and points us to our future. We can be assured that while we can know God's Spirit now, we will also live in his presence forever.

Prayer: *Dear God, help us see that you care for us so much that you placed your Spirit in us as a guarantee that we will be with you forever. Amen*

Thought for the day: God's Spirit in my heart is a reminder of greater things to come.

Zack Carden (Georgia, US)

God listens

Read Ephesians 6:18–20

The prayer of a righteous person is powerful and effective.
James 5:16 (NIV)

In February 2016 I was sentenced to time in prison, a new and unexpected experience for me, after having served my country as a soldier and my community as a firefighter. In June 2017, I began sharing a cell with an older man who explained to me the message of the gospel. Seven days later, I accepted Jesus as my Saviour. As my cellmate and I prayed and studied each day, I began to experience God's love in amazing ways.

My new friend gave me a Bible with James 5:16 highlighted. The next day he was told he would be transferred to another prison, so we both prayed fervently that he would not be moved. The day he was to leave, the transfer was cancelled. But then, three weeks later, my friend was sent to another prison. Instead of being angry with God for separating us, I kept reading his word and prayed constantly that it would be his will to bring us back together again.

Twelve days later, he and I were both transferred – to the same prison – and we were cellmates once again. God truly answered our prayers in the way that we had hoped. Now we have a daily fellowship group with several other inmates. Every time our group is together, we pray for each other.

Prayer: *Faithful God, whenever we are lost and depressed from our trials, give us strength. Amen*

Thought for the day: Every day, I pray for the Lord's will to be done.

Aaron Priest (New South Wales, Australia)

We of little faith

Read Mark 5:24–34

My message and my preaching [were] presented… with a demonstration of the Spirit and of power… so that your faith might not depend on the wisdom of people but on the power of God.
1 Corinthians 2:4–5 (CEB)

When my aunt was being tested for a life-threatening illness, I started praying desperately that if she had the illness she would be healed. I worried, though, that my faith needed to be rock solid for God to hear me, and I didn't believe my faith was that strong.

Then I remembered the story of the woman who had bled for years and who reached out of the crowd to touch Jesus' clothes, believing she would be healed. Jesus commended her for her faith and then healed her. We often view this woman as having ultimate faith. However, over the twelve years before she came to Jesus, this woman had exhausted every other option. When she reached out, she was desperate. All she had left was her belief in Jesus' power to heal her.

The idea of a huge faith is intimidating. We wonder how we can possibly have faith big enough to face the major issues in our lives. But Jesus tells us, 'If you have faith as small as a mustard seed, you can say to this mountain, "Move from here to there," and it will move. Nothing will be impossible for you' (Matthew 17:20, NIV). This verse helps me to see that it is never about the size of our faith, but rather the size of God's power. In any situation Jesus will hear us when we cry out to him.

Prayer: *Dear Lord, help us to reach out to you in any circumstance, knowing you will hear us. Amen*

Thought for the day: God's power is greater than anything I go through.

Dorcas Buckley (Washington, US)

PRAYER FOCUS: SOMEONE AWAITING A DIAGNOSIS

Steadfast

Read Romans 12:9–13

Seek first [your heavenly Father's] kingdom and his righteousness, and all these things will be given to you as well.
Matthew 6:33 (NIV)

When I was younger, I played golf two or three times a week with friends. And I was fairly competitive. When I had an especially good game, I would expect my next game to be even better. However, usually the next game would turn out to be one of my worst games of the year. I believe I focused on the good score I was going to achieve rather than giving my full attention to each shot I needed to make. Good golfers must constantly remind themselves to keep their eye on the ball to deliver each shot.

In our service to the Lord, it is even more important to avoid becoming distracted. Daily demands can divert our attention from our relationship with God, and ambitions can distract us from our purpose. In today's scripture reading Paul calls us to be steadfast in prayer, which will help us to keep our eye on fulfilling our commitment to God.

Prayer: *Dear Lord, help us to persevere in prayer and service to you and to others. Amen*

Thought for the day: Today I will remain focused on what God has called me to do.

Walter N. Maris (Missouri, US)

No regrets

Several years ago I was walking into town for dinner one evening, when a man approached me on the pavement. He said that he was hungry and asked me to buy him food. I told him that maybe I could help him on my way back. I continued on my way, ate my supper, paid the bill and returned to my car by a different route so that I wouldn't have to encounter him again.

I am ashamed to say that I didn't give the man a second thought that night. But I have given him a second thought since. I have never forgotten the incident, and to this day it remains a painful memory. It was not one of my finer moments. Whenever the memory surfaces, I find myself wondering what happened to the man. Did anyone give him something to eat? I think about what I would do differently if I could do it again.

I would like to be able to say that this is the only time I have passed by someone in need; but it isn't. I have done the same since – kept on going when I could have helped, had the means to help and had every reason in the world to help. I think about the apostle Paul, shipwrecked on the island of Malta. He says of the people he encountered there that they showed him 'unusual kindness' (Acts 28:2, NIV). I find 'unusual kindness' a striking turn of phrase. Their kindness to Paul was rare, unexpected, not required and perhaps inconvenient; but they still went out of their way to care for him. Unfortunately, the man whose need I ignored could not say the same of me.

I am reminded of times in my own life when others have shown me unusual kindness. Nine times out of ten, it is the smallest acts that have made the most difference – an encouraging word when I really needed it, an invitation to dinner when I was feeling lonely; the list goes on. These actions have made a lasting impression on me and changed the way that I am attentive to, and respond to, the needs of others. I do my best not only to help when called on but to look for situations in which the need may be less obvious.

My mother is always saying that she wants to have no regrets when given the opportunity to show her faith through her actions. When she has the chance to offer help, show kindness, compassion or gratitude, she takes it. 'No regrets' has also become a mantra for me.

Sometimes we have opportunities to display our faith in grand and spectacular ways. But more often we can show it through small and simple acts of kindness, compassion and service – visiting an elderly person in a nursing home, cutting the grass for our neighbour who is recovering from surgery, buying food for someone who is hungry. Now when I encounter an opportunity – big or small – to put my faith into action, I remind myself of the night I passed by someone in need. I remind myself that when it comes to helping others, I want to have no more regrets.

Several meditations in this issue address putting our faith into action. You may want to read again the meditations for 2, 18, 26, 29 September; 5, 8, 12, 21, 25 October; 3, 15, 21, 26, 28 November; and 5, 15, 22 and 29 December before responding to the reflection questions below.

QUESTIONS FOR REFLECTION

1 When have you missed an opportunity to put your faith into action? What will you do differently the next time you have a similar opportunity?

2 Read Hebrews 13:2. Recall a time when you have seen this verse lived out in a real way. What did you observe? What did this experience teach you about how we are to help others?

3 How can you help others in small and simple ways in the coming week?

Andrew Garland Breeden
Acquisitions Editor

Godly inspiration

Read Hebrews 11:1–12

Let us run with perseverance the race marked out for us.
Hebrews 12:1 (NIV)

In today's reading, the writer of Hebrews cites the lives and labours of many Old Testament heroes – people like Gideon, David and Joseph. Despite the challenges and trials they faced, these people stepped out in faith. God was with them, and they persevered. The opening verses of chapter 12 are an exhortation to follow their example.

One of the best ways to energise our Christian lives is to ponder the lives of godly men and women who have gone before us. We don't have to go back to the Old Testament to find examples of great faith. I have poignant memories of people whose vibrant faith inspired me.

One friend, after receiving a diagnosis of cancer with six months to live, did not bemoan his fate but found strength in Christ's presence and promises. Another friend – in the face of job loss, her husband's illness and her mother's death – chose to commit her time to prayer and reading the Bible, which sustained her and inspired others. Most of us can name someone who has shown us an example of great faith in the face of trials. They bear witness to us that God can see us through, no matter how trying our circumstances.

Prayer: *Dear Lord, thank you for the faithful ones who have gone before us. Grant us courage to follow their examples. Amen*

Thought for the day: Who has been an example of great faith to me?

Wayne Greenawalt (Illinois, US)

Heavy burdens

Read Psalm 46

The God of all grace, who has called you to his eternal glory in Christ, will himself restore, support, strengthen, and establish you.
1 Peter 5:10 (NRSV)

As I was going through the difficult end of a marriage and moving into the even-more-challenging role of a single parent, I became an expert in hiding my emotions. In public I pretended to be confident and cheerful while in reality I was full of self-doubt, depressed and drained.

At first I was able to express my true feelings only during times of prayer when my words were flooded by tears of anger, anxiety and aggravation. Eventually, I acknowledged that I was unable to handle things alone and allowed God to carry my burdens. This happened through sharing with trusted friends at church who were experiencing similar situations, engaging in weekly conversations with a Christian therapist and adopting a healthier lifestyle through improved nutrition and regular exercise. God faithfully continued to love, encourage and walk beside me every moment of every day, and I experienced the rest and renewal I so desperately needed.

Hiding our true feelings is exhausting and doesn't really help a troubling situation. Letting go and allowing God to carry our heavy burdens does help. God loves each of us. As we read the Bible and devote time to prayer, we can sense his presence with us – giving us strength and rest.

Prayer: *Loving God, may we always be aware of your closeness and willingness to carry our burdens. Amen*

Thought for the day: When I let go of control, I begin to see the way God can lighten my load.

Jill Maisch (Maryland, US)

Sharing

Read Matthew 14:13–21

In the midst of a very severe trial, [the Macedonian churches']
overflowing joy and their extreme poverty welled up in rich generosity.
2 Corinthians 8:2 (NIV)

A fire spread quickly through the flats, and the entire building was almost completely destroyed. Over 80 people died in the blaze. Hundreds had become homeless, many left standing in the street – all their possessions gone. Long before the flames had been extinguished, people from the surrounding area had gathered and were offering food, clothing and comfort. Some even offered shelter.

The authorities were slow to respond, so it was largely left to neighbours and non-profit organisations to relieve want and suffering. Like the Macedonians in today's reading, most of the people living in that area did not have much themselves, but they were willing to share what they had with others.

We can never assume that someone else will help or that people can cope in difficult circumstances. In the story of Jesus feeding the five thousand, the disciples asked Jesus to send the people away to buy food when they became hungry. But instead, Jesus said, 'You give them something to eat' (Matthew 14:16). Andrew responded by bringing to Jesus a boy who was willing to share his lunch (see John 6:8–9). Each of us can be that boy when we act as God's hands and feet to bring solace to those who are hurting.

Prayer: *Dear Lord, give us this day our daily bread, and grant us the grace to share it with others. Amen*

Thought for the day: Today I will share with others what God has given me.

Bill Findlay (Scotland)

Created for God's purpose

Read 1 Corinthians 12:18–27

We are the clay, and you are our potter. All of us are the work of your hand.
Isaiah 64:8 (CEB)

Every November our women's group hosts a coffee morning and cake sale to raise money for local missions. Our cake sales bring together the different generations in our church to work as one body. This year I decided to bake cookies and brownies and as I prepared my items to bake, I remembered that I am the work of God's hands. Just as I mould my ingredients together, God moulds me for his purpose. We are created in God's image and equipped for the work of the kingdom (see Ephesians 4:12).

When I don't feel equipped, I can rely on God's strength and not my own. We can serve in many ways, both big and small. Each one of us has a part, whether it's raising money by having a church cake sale, writing a devotional meditation or going into the mission field. As we grow in our walk with God, our faith grows and he gives us a longing to serve in new ways.

Prayer: *Dear God, thank you for moulding us into your image to do your work. Show each of us how we can serve your kingdom today. As Jesus taught us, we pray, 'Our Father in heaven, hallowed be your name, your kingdom come, your will be done, on earth as it is in heaven. Give us today our daily bread. And forgive us our debts, as we also have forgiven our debtors. And lead us not into temptation, but deliver us from the evil one.'* Amen*

Thought for the day: God will equip me for works of service.

Julie Wicker (South Carolina, US)

PRAYER FOCUS: LOCAL MISSIONS
*Matthew 6:9–13 (NIV)

Words of peace

Read Colossians 4:2–6

Let your conversation be always full of grace, seasoned with salt, so that you may know how to answer everyone.
Colossians 4:6 (NIV)

The businessman in the queue behind me at the post office had a plane to catch. When others waiting in line began to grumble about the slow service, he said, 'It's really not that bad; I'm sure I'll make my flight.' The conversation turned to poor airline service and surly transport staff. The businessman demurred. 'I fly for business every week. My flights are almost always on time. The staff are great.' He began to entertain us with stories about his travels.

When my turn at the counter came, I stepped back and told him to go ahead of me. 'No need,' he said. 'I insist,' I replied. After he had posted his package, he turned to hand me a gift – a bright-red rubber giraffe with his company logo on it.

In Colossians 4:6 Paul urges, 'Let your conversation be always full of grace, seasoned with salt, so that you may know how to answer everyone.' Our words matter. By redirecting the conversation, the businessman turned critical spirits into appreciative hearts. The cheerful giraffe stands on my desk to remind me always to choose words of peace.

Prayer: *Dear Lord, thank you for teaching us that peaceful words and compassionate deeds are a powerful witness. Help us recognise opportunities to plant seeds of peace. Amen*

Thought for the day: I want the words I speak to be full of grace (see Colossians 4:6).

Sydney Avey (California, US)

Spiritual myopia

Read 1 Samuel 16:1–13

The Lord does not look at the things people look at. People look at the outward appearance, but the Lord looks at the heart.
1 Samuel 16:7 (NIV)

I was diagnosed with myopia and astigmatism a few years ago. Fellow sufferers know how difficult it is to depend on wearing glasses, but without glasses, everything is blurred and hard to distinguish. I can see someone in the distance and not recognise who it is, which can be frustrating and sad.

Sometimes we also suffer from spiritual myopia – blinkers that keep us from seeing beyond our self-righteousness, prejudices and stereotypes. We may label people or condemn them for past mistakes. Jesus, however, saw the human condition of people from every walk of life and treated them all with love and mercy. Tax collectors and prostitutes were treated with equal respect. Because of the way Jesus treated others, he gained their genuine love and trust.

As followers of Christ, we are called to witness to all people and to reach out to them, regardless of their condition. After all, Christ fixed his eyes on us when we were not at our best and redeemed us with love and grace.

Prayer: *Dear Lord, remove our blinkers and help us to see people as you do, with love and compassion. Amen*

Thought for the day: God cares most about what is in my heart.

Narda Luz Vargas Guerrero (Dominican Republic)

Forgiveness

Read Luke 6:32–36

Neither height nor depth, nor anything else in all creation, will be able to separate us from the love of God that is in Christ Jesus our Lord.
Romans 8:39 (NIV)

At the age of 14 I endured six months of bullying by a classmate. I flinched when her slimy spit hit my face, when her fingers jabbed my back on bus rides after school and when she called me names. When she began harassing me with hateful phone calls at home, my parents had a restraining order placed on her.

Jesus told us to bless those who curse us and to pray for those who abuse us (see Luke 6:28). I knew that Jesus forgave those who crucified him, yet I wasn't sure how to forgive my bully. My parents encouraged me to get involved at church. I volunteered in the crèche, where I learned to focus less on my hurt and more on other people's needs.

My heart was prepared to listen when a close friend told me that, to know true peace of mind, I needed to forgive the girl. My friend helped me to see the way to do this: to think of that girl with Jesus. As I struggled to speak the words, 'I forgive her', I imagined Jesus embracing her.

Now whenever I think of the girl, I picture her in Jesus' arms. I realise that she needs God's love too. God accepts us and loves us, and that love changes brokenness into wholeness.

Prayer: *Merciful God, thank you for your amazing love. Help us to forgive others and show them your love. Amen*

Thought for the day: Nothing can separate me from God's love.

Stephanie Brown (Kansas, US)

Love and provision

Read 1 John 3:11–24

Let us not love with words or speech but with actions and in truth.
1 John 3:18 (NIV)

During my second pregnancy, my husband and I moved to a different area of the country. In the first few months, since so much around me was new and I was not working, many days with my toddler felt lonely and long. When we found a church through some friends, we decided to join the small group that met in their home. Three days after the first meeting, our beautiful daughter was born. The next few weeks were hard as I tried to balance time with my toddler while also handling the demands of a new baby. By 6.00 pm every day I was in tears, wondering how I would get through the following day.

But something wonderful happened. People from our small group, many of whom we had only met at that first meeting, turned up at our door with home-cooked meals. They brought with them not only delicious food but also the aroma of Christ. They showed love to us in our chaos, even though they hardly knew us. Some of them were in the middle of major problems themselves, yet they still sacrificed and cared for our family in this way. Their actions reminded us that Jesus often shows his love and provision through people who choose not only to hear the word but to be doers of it as well. What a blessing!

Prayer: *Dear God, thank you for sending people into our lives who show us your love when we need it most. In Jesus' name. Amen*

Thought for the day: How can I share the aroma of Christ with others today?

Courtney Boulware (Ohio, US)

Consistent faith

Read Romans 8:35–39

Do not be afraid; do not be discouraged, for the Lord your God will be with you wherever you go.
Joshua 1:9 (NIV)

Last year my father, my only immediate family member nearby, was deported to Mexico after living in the United States for nearly 40 years. I had lived with him for most of my life, and he was suddenly gone. Because I was living in a hall of residence at my university, I wasn't entirely homeless; but my only outside support had disappeared.

The next months of my life were very stressful. I would ask myself questions like, 'Where will I be living in a few months?' and 'Where will I stay during the holidays?' My emotional state declined and so did my university work.

One day, a friend's parents telephoned and said they wanted to talk to me. We met for dinner, and they explained that they were feeling called to help me. At that moment I felt as if a two-ton weight had been lifted off my back.

I realised then that my situation had always been in God's hands, but I had let my emotions fall into a deep hole. God knew the outcome from the beginning and already had a plan to take care of me. During my struggle, I forgot that he is always with us. I see now that if we walk with the Lord and put all our faith in him, then we do not need to worry.

Prayer: *Dear Lord, help us to be more confident in our faith in you, especially as we endure struggles. Amen*

Thought for the day: God is by my side at all times.

Ivan Hernandez (Texas, US)

Trust

Read Psalm 36:5–7

[Jesus said,] 'Truly I tell you, whoever does not receive the kingdom of God as a little child will never enter it.'
Luke 18:17 (NRSV)

One day last summer, I decided to go swimming. It was a windy day with few people on the beach – only some surfers enjoying the waves. I admired their skill and bravery. When one of the surfboards came closer to me, I was amazed to see a young boy sitting on it holding on to his father's legs. He did not seem afraid; he smiled and looked quite happy. I was impressed by the young boy's trust in his father. He was calm floating on the waves because his father was close to him.

In the sea of life, we can be calm and even take pleasure when we keep hold of our heavenly Father. Jesus tells us to have faith like a child. Whether we are happy or in tears, God loves us, and we can trust that he will calm our fears and keep hold of us always.

Prayer: *Heavenly Father, thank you for being with us in every moment of our lives. Help us to focus not on our fears but on you. Amen*

Thought for the day: Trusting God is reason enough to be joyful.

Lidiya Petrova (Varna, Bulgaria)

Celebrate

Read Hebrews 13:5–8

Rejoice in the Lord always. I will say it again: rejoice!
Philippians 4:4 (NIV)

Recently, my mother went home to be with the Lord. Even though she lived her 83 years to the fullest, my heart was still broken. I wanted her funeral to emulate the bright and courageous way she enjoyed life – so we followed her three simple instructions: no black clothes, only happy stories and, if possible, only tears of joy.

I searched for a way to pay my respects to Mum that would honour her wishes but also be a unique example of my love for her. Feeling overwhelmed, I turned to God. The answer to my prayers came in the form of a small stone. I discovered that I could order decorative river rocks with different inscriptions: Love, Hope, Faith and so on. The word I decided on was Celebrate, because it seemed the perfect embodiment of a life well lived.

On the day of the funeral, I spoke about the stones as part of the eulogy. At the gathering afterwards, people asked me about the inscribed stones. Family and friends loved the idea that they could have a tangible reminder of Mum and celebrate her forever. I still miss my mother every day. But I carry my stone with me and draw additional strength from Hebrews 13:5: '[God] will never leave you or forsake you' (NRSV).

Prayer: *Heavenly Father, thank you for loving us today, tomorrow and always. Amen*

Thought for the day: Because of God's love, we can celebrate every moment of life.

Kevin Evelyn (Florida, US)

PRAYER FOCUS: SOMEONE MOURNING THE DEATH OF A PARENT

The 'God Box'

Read Matthew 11:28–30
Cast all your anxiety on [God] because he cares for you.
1 Peter 5:7 (NIV)

A retired builder and cabinet maker, my brother Lee had a carpentry shop in his garden and continued to work there after being diagnosed with terminal cancer. For years he had made unique items for community groups to sell at fundraising events. One of his most popular was a small box made of beautiful cherry wood with a brass plate on top reading 'God Box'. There was a note inside, instructing the recipient to put all their worries and cares in the God Box and leave them there.

While the concept of a God Box did not originate with Lee, he made a ministry of building his version and giving away hundreds of them. In the weeks before his death, he made more than a dozen boxes and put them out for family and friends to take. On the day he died, he asked that one be given to his hospice nurse and the chaplain who came to visit. 'This gift will be the focus of my Sunday sermon,' the chaplain said.

During his final hours, a sweet, peaceful serenity washed over Lee as his family kept vigil at his bedside. Lifelong friends came to say goodbye. As word came that Lee had quietly slipped away, they left with tears in their eyes and – for those who did not already have one – a God Box in their hands.

Prayer: *Dear Lord, grant us the courage to trust you with all our worries and fears. Amen*

Thought for the day: What talent can I use to show God's love to others?

Luleen S. Anderson (North Carolina, US)

Letting go

Read Deuteronomy 33:1–12

God is our refuge and strength, an ever-present help in trouble.
Therefore we will not fear.
Psalm 46:1–2 (NIV)

It was almost noon, and I was anxious. I was waiting to see if I was going to get a delivery of shingles medication that has to be started soon after an outbreak to be effective. I don't drive, and the delivery service has a noon deadline. Waiting and uncertainty trigger post-traumatic stress disorder (PTSD) in me.

I stared past the cacti and Joshua trees to the mountains in the distance. Suddenly, it occurred to me that God would take care of me. I wrote the name of the medicine on a slip of paper and put it in my 'God Box', a box that serves as a physical reminder to give my worries to God.

A short time later, I received a call saying that the medicine would be delivered that day. But even before that call, I felt more peaceful because I had let go of my worry and had faith that God would help one way or another.

My pastor says, 'Victory is not the absence of struggle. It is the presence of God in your struggle.' Although I wish I didn't struggle with PTSD, I'm grateful that God helps me get through it. We may struggle to trust God in uncertain situations, but when we surrender our worries to God, God can heal us and provide for us.

Prayer: *Dear God, help us to trust in you when we feel anxious. Thank you for giving us peace even when we worry. Amen*

Thought for the day: When I give my worries to God, I can find peace.

(Ms) Loe Griffith (Arizona, US)

God provides

Read Luke 9:1–6
[Jesus] said to them, 'Take nothing for your journey, no staff, nor bag, nor bread, nor money – not even an extra tunic.'
Luke 9:3 (NRSV)

In today's passage, Jesus sends out the twelve disciples to teach and heal. I believe we are all called to follow Jesus' command by sharing the gospel and leading others to salvation. But I still have many concerns: my family's well-being, my livelihood as a minister, and my family and community's economic situation. As a minister, I am very concerned about how we budget our money, and I have to decide how much goes towards evangelism.

Recently, an organisation asked me to serve God through their ministry to teach underprivileged children about music and about the message of Jesus Christ. The organisation paid all my expenses and supported the children I served with clothing, food, travel expenses and school supplies. But in the six months I worked there, I still had concerns about whether I was serving well and following Jesus' command to the disciples.

No matter how we serve, we are called to share Jesus' message of salvation for all. When we take part in God's ministry, we can have faith in his promises. When we dedicate our life to God's work, we do not need to worry. He prepares us to serve.

Prayer: *Dear God, help us to trust in you as we do your will. In Jesus' name. Amen*

Thought for the day: God provides for me when I respond to his call.

Manus Thepjunta (Phrae, Thailand)

Faithful in service

Read Matthew 21:28–32

The father went to the other son and said the same thing. He answered, 'I will, sir,' but he did not go.
Matthew 21:30 (NIV)

'Bob's celebrating his 90th birthday next week,' I remarked to my husband. 'I could get him a card and bake him something. He's been so lonely since his wife went into care.' We had enjoyed Bob and his wife as our neighbours for 37 years. Regrettably, I never got around to getting a card or baking – I missed an opportunity to show kindness.

This experience reminds me of the parable Jesus told in Matthew 21. The first son refused to work, but later did the job. The second son agreed to work, but never did. Jesus asked his listeners, 'Which son did his father's will?' The correct answer is the first son.

Did the second son deliberately break his word or did he simply procrastinate? Perhaps he meant to go but just never got around to it. I want to be like the son who obeyed his father, but sadly I more often procrastinate. I know I have been called to be fruitful and helpful, to worship regularly and to spend time in prayer. I mean to do it – but frequently I put it off. How often have I procrastinated and missed opportunities to show Christian kindness? This parable is a reminder to follow through on our good intentions in our faithful service to Christ.

Prayer: *Loving God, open our eyes to opportunities to serve, and give us the motivation and energy to follow through. Amen*

Thought for the day: How am I procrastinating in serving God?

Cheryl A. Paden (Nebraska, US)

Guide our steps

Read 2 Samuel 22:1–7

In my distress I called to the Lord; I cried to my God for help. From his temple he heard my voice; my cry came before him, into his ears.
Psalm 18:6 (NIV)

A few months after my graduation from college, I found myself running to find a safe place to hide. My native country had broken out into a war that killed approximately 800,000 people – including my family members. This unexpected, barbaric event left me parentless, homeless and penniless. I began to wonder where my God had been when these horrible things were happening. I found myself in a state of confusion, not knowing where and how to move forward in life.

I remember one day sitting under a tree having a conversation with God. 'God, please hear me. How will I move forward? How can I survive as an orphan, without support and guidance? Who will comfort me? Who will counsel me? Who will provide for me?' I felt paralysed with fear and grief.

Sometimes we face challenges beyond our control. Psalm 18:6 reminds us to call on the Lord for help in times of distress, and he will hear our prayers. Knowing that God hears our cries and is with us every step we take gave me strength in the darkest hours of my life. We can trust that regardless of what life throws at us, God hears our prayers and will guide our steps.

Prayer: *Dear God, help us to lean on you and to trust you in times of fear and grief. In Jesus' name, we pray. Amen*

Thought for the day: God hears my deepest cries.

Clementine M. Msengi (Texas, US)

Our prime meridian

Read Isaiah 43:5–7

I am the Alpha and the Omega, the Beginning and the End. To the thirsty I will give water without cost from the spring of the water of life.
Revelation 21:6 (NIV)

On a ministry trip, I stopped in London and spent a day at the Greenwich Observatory, from which all time zones of the world are measured: Greenwich Mean Time (GMT). It's where all maps and GPS coordinates begin, zero degrees longitude. Outside the observatory, a thick red line – along the Greenwich Prime Meridian – emblazons the ground for tourists to take pictures with one foot in the Western Hemisphere and one foot in the Eastern Hemisphere, thus being in two places at once.

After arriving in Ghana and touring the port city of Tema, I was stunned and delighted to learn that the prime meridian slices right through the city, precisely 4,400 miles south of Greenwich, and that a church sits directly upon it: the Presbyterian Church of the Greenwich Meridian. For a long time I stood before that church, thinking about Christ – our Alpha and Omega – our beginning and end.

When we have lost our bearings, our courage and our vision, and cannot see the way ahead, we can turn to our Saviour, our Source and our Destination. In Christ, east and west meet. He is the place where we were first loved and baptised, the place where we were first called and empowered to go forth and serve.

Prayer: *Dear Jesus, align our inner spiritual compass that we may be faithful. Amen*

Thought for the day: God is both my source and my destination.

Hope Harle-Mould (New York, US)

Servant heart

Read John 13:3–17

Whatever you do, whether in word or deed, do it all in the name of the Lord Jesus.
Colossians 3:17 (NIV)

For six weeks my broken knee had limited my ability to do things for myself. When my friend offered to come over and care for my feet, I reluctantly accepted. She arrived and promptly began by filling a basin with warm water to soak my feet. After that she sat and tenderly dried them, clipped and filed the nails, and finally polished the nails to make me feel pampered.

My friend's act of service reminded me of Jesus washing his disciples' feet. He was their teacher and their Lord but he took on a task reserved for household servants. He taught in words and by example how they should treat one another. Paul expressed it this way: 'Do nothing out of selfish ambition or vain conceit. Rather, in humility value others above yourselves, not looking to your own interests but each of you to the interests of the others' (Philippians 2:3–4).

I was humbled by my friend's servant heart and challenged by scripture and by her example to look for those in need. I want to seek ways – no matter how humble – that I can serve God by serving others.

Prayer: *Dear God, help us to be mindful of the needs of others. Amen*

Thought for the day: Jesus is my example for serving others.

Carol Harrison (Saskatchewan, Canada)

Clear conscience

Read James 5:13–16

I preached that they should repent and turn to God and demonstrate their repentance by their deeds.
Acts 26:20 (NIV)

When I walked into the garage, I asked to speak to the owner about a personal matter. Palms sweating and stomach churning, I went into his office. 'I'm a thief,' I blurted out. 'I stole a car from your business several years ago. Now God has convicted me. I need to ask for forgiveness and to make restitution.'

At first, the owner stood frozen. Then a large smile spread across his face. Bolting around his desk, he grabbed my hand and said, 'I forgive you. And as for paying me back for the car, the insurance took care of that years ago.' He paused and added, 'You know, my children have been talking to me about Jesus too.'

After becoming a Christian at college, I felt challenged by Paul to keep a good conscience (see 1 Timothy 1:19). My first stop was the car garage. It was difficult to confess my sin, but I left that office feeling as if I was floating two feet off the ground. That encounter gave me the faith and strength to ask others for forgiveness. There's nothing like laying your head down to sleep at night and knowing that your conscience is clear before God.

Prayer: *Dear God, thank you for your grace. May we have the strength and faith to set things right so that we may live with a clear conscience. Amen*

Thought for the day: A clear conscience gives me peace with God.

James Smith (California, US)

Out of the back window

Read Isaiah 43:16–21

[The Lord says,] 'Forget the former things; do not dwell on the past. See, I am doing a new thing!'
Isaiah 43:18–19 (NIV)

My dog, Ranger, was sitting in the passenger seat of my truck as I was driving down a country road on a summer afternoon. After a while I drove past a rabbit sitting beside the road. When Ranger saw the rabbit, he began barking and turned to look through the back window to watch it. Even after the rabbit was far out of sight, Ranger continued looking through the back window.

Meanwhile, two more rabbits darted across the road ahead of us; however, because Ranger was still focused on the first rabbit, he never saw the others. Seeing two rabbits running across the road and into the field would have brought him much more excitement than seeing a single rabbit sitting by the road.

This experience made me wonder how many of God's blessings I have missed because, like Ranger, I am occupied with things of the past instead of looking forward in anticipation of what God has planned for me. Continuing to focus on past events, whether they are joyous or devastating, can prevent us from seeing the blessings God has in store for our future.

Prayer: *Dear Father, help bring us closure from things in the past that have prevented us from moving forwards. Open our eyes to the blessings you provide, and help us always to remain focused on the future. Amen*

Thought for the day: I can rest in the hope that new days will bring God's new blessings.

Kendra Jacobs (New Mexico, US)

PRAYER FOCUS: SOMEONE TRYING TO LET GO OF THE PAST

God's love

Read John 15:9–17

[Jesus said,] 'You did not choose me, but I chose you and appointed you so that you might go and bear… fruit that will last… This is my command: love each other.'
John 15:16–17 (NIV)

When I decided to leave my job, I was able to open my house to any of the mountain-village children who wanted to learn English and mathematics for free. First only one child, Imam, came. One day he asked me, 'Why do you teach me for free?' I replied that I wanted to share what I have learned. Then he asked, 'Why do you want to share with me?' I replied, 'Because I love you.'

When he asked me why I loved him, I said, 'Because God has loved me first.' The next day, he came with three friends. Then a few days later, he came with another two friends and the next day with six new friends. When I asked him why he kept bringing new students, he said, 'Because you loved me first, Ma'am.'

Jesus said, 'Love each other as I have loved you' (John 15:12). God's love will enable us to love others and share with them in our own limited ways. My heart is full of joy when I share God's love with my students. Some people say that teaching them is a waste of time since I'm not getting paid. But my joy does not come from what others think and say. My eternal joy comes from God, who has loved me and who will provide what I need and more to share with others.

Prayer: *Dear God, help us to love each other and share your love with others. Amen*

Thought for the day: With whom can I share God's love today?

Linda Chandra (Banten, Indonesia)

Growing in Christ

Read Psalm 92:12–15

Jesus increased in wisdom and in years, and in divine and human favour.

Luke 2:52 (NRSV)

Recently, when I visited the fields that my grandfather had farmed, I had a big surprise. Expecting to see open fields, I walked into a forest of giant pine trees. The fields where he used to plant soya beans more than 50 years ago had been transformed into a forest of trees that were 100 feet high.

God's natural process of sowing seedlings from surrounding trees had started new growth in the once-open fields. The soil was rich in nutrients and the natural water supply was more than adequate. The seedlings had grown into saplings, and the saplings had become mature trees.

This experience reminded me of how we as God's children can grow. Luke describes such growth when he writes that Jesus grew 'in wisdom and in years, and in divine and human favour'. I am grateful to my parents, who planted in me the seed of Jesus Christ. Our Christian faith community also provides for us rich soil in which we can grow, nurtured by the Father, the Son and the Holy Spirit. I am grateful too that the foundation of our spiritual growth is simply God's abundant grace.

Prayer: *Nurturing God, we praise you and thank you for your grace that provides for our spiritual growth. May we seek every opportunity to continue to grow in the likeness of Jesus Christ. Amen*

Thought for the day: As I seek spiritual growth, God will transform me into the likeness of Christ.

Ernest S. Lyght (New Jersey, US)

Even me

Read 1 Timothy 1:12–17

Christ Jesus came into the world to save sinners – of whom I am the worst.
1 Timothy 1:15 (NIV)

I didn't become a Christian until I was 32 years old. Until that time I did not know God. Looking back on my youth and young adult life, I feel shame for some of the things I did. I was a selfish young man; I had only my earthly desires on my mind.

I can relate to Paul's words to Timothy in 1 Timothy 1:15. Paul, who persecuted Christ's followers until the point of his own conversion to the Christian faith, felt that he was the worst sinner there could be. However, in God's eyes, sin is sin and it does not matter how we rank it here on earth. Paul said, 'For all have sinned and fall short of the glory of God' (Romans 3:23). What does matter is that we have accepted Jesus Christ as our Lord and Saviour. Paul, led by the Holy Spirit, went on to accomplish many tasks for Jesus Christ, including writing many of the books in the New Testament. If Jesus can use Paul in such a remarkable way, then he can use each of us too.

Prayer: *Lord Jesus, help us to use our gifts and talents to further your kingdom. In Jesus' name, we pray. Amen*

Thought for the day: How will I use my talents for God's kingdom?

Nathan Reid (Maine, US)

Interruptions

Read Hebrews 12:1–3

The Lord came and stood there, calling as at the other times, 'Samuel! Samuel!' Then Samuel said, 'Speak, for your servant is listening.'
1 Samuel 3:10 (NIV)

'Julia!' A voice hailed me as I emerged on to the street from the dentist's office. My friend and I exchanged greetings. Suddenly, birds began singing: her phone ringtone. She reached into her pocket and pulled out her phone. The singing stopped as she proceeded to read a text. 'Is the family okay?' I asked after a moment. My friend nodded as her fingers flew over the phone keypad. After a few minutes, I gave up trying to regain her attention. 'Cheerio, then,' I said and left. As I crossed the road she was still texting on her phone.

I suddenly thought, 'Is that how we are with God?' On many occasions my quiet time with God has been interrupted in some way by the phone ringing, a knock at the door, family in a hurry or suddenly remembering an item to add to the shopping list. It's all too easy to become distracted. Although our attention sometimes slips from God, his focus on us never wavers.

Prayer: *Forgive us, Lord, when we let less important matters distract us from you. Help us to focus on you and cherish our time in your presence. Amen*

Thought for the day: I always have God's attention.

Julia Cutting (North Yorkshire, England)

Renewed strength

Read 2 Corinthians 1:3–7

[God] comforts us in all our troubles, so that we can comfort those in any trouble with the comfort we ourselves receive from God.
2 Corinthians 1:4 (NIV)

I was deeply saddened when I received the news that a good friend from our congregation had died of cancer. This brought back memories of the deaths of my mother and sister after their struggles with terminal disease. I could not hold back my tears.

My three-year-old son came over to me, caressed my face and asked, 'What's wrong, Mummy? Why are you crying?' I told him, 'I miss my mother and my sister.' He looked at me and smiled, then took my hand and pulled me outside into the garden. He said, 'Look at the sky, Mummy. They are there with God. God is taking care of them. You don't need to be sad.'

God was there in that moment, showing me the power and breadth of faith. My son was witnessing to the faithfulness of God being with us in this life and in life beyond death. That conversation with my son renewed my strength and helped me move ahead, acknowledging that God sometimes uses ways beyond our understanding to demonstrate his love and mercy.

Prayer: *God of everlasting love, help us to persevere in our faith journey. Amen*

Thought for the day: God renews me in unexpected ways.

Angieluz Valle Rodríguez (Puerto Rico)

Our treasure

Read Matthew 6:19–24

Where your treasure is, there your heart will be also.
Matthew 6:21 (NIV)

I stopped at my uncle's garage and shop to buy some petrol and went inside to pay. As usual the shop was busy with people buying groceries and other items they needed in the small southern town. My uncle was busy writing down the customers' purchases on a carbon copy receipt book which he placed in a Coca-Cola delivery box bulging with receipts. He allowed customers to buy from him on credit, and he never tried to collect from those who owed money. Many of his customers were in dire need of help and knew about my uncle's generosity. My uncle would often open the store on a Sunday or a holiday to provide medicine or groceries for a family that needed help, and he never complained.

I told my uncle that his business could do much better if he asked for cash or a credit card when people bought things. He told me that he was 'building treasures in heaven and not on this earth'. Every time I see an old Coca-Cola box, I think of my uncle who built his treasures in heaven, not on earth. He is in heaven now and enjoying the treasures he stored up there, and I will always remember the lesson he taught me.

Prayer: *Dear God, help us to remember to build our treasures in heaven, not in this world. Amen*

Thought for the day: I will store up treasures in heaven by helping those in need.

Barry Wright (Georgia, US)

God's care

Read Psalm 91:1–13

He will command his angels concerning you to guard you in all your ways.
Psalm 91:11 (NIV)

One day in November 2017 my daughter was in a serious car accident while on her way to work. She was terribly injured and became unconscious. A few strangers who witnessed the accident called an ambulance, and it seemed as though those helpful strangers were God's angels. Descriptions of the accident were shocking, but we thank God for miraculously saving our daughter. She received proper treatment and over time made a remarkable recovery.

We recognise God's care when we walk in close proximity with him. My family prays together every day, and we had prayed on that November morning before my daughter left for work. While my daughter was recovering, we had many visits from people who shared their concern and encouragement. Our God is faithful.

Prayer: *God, our protector, thank you for watching over us. Help us to remain close to you. We pray as Jesus taught us, 'Our Father which art in heaven, Hallowed be thy name. Thy kingdom come, Thy will be done in earth, as it is in heaven. Give us this day our daily bread. And forgive us our debts, as we forgive our debtors. And lead us not into temptation, but deliver us from evil: For thine is the kingdom, and the power, and the glory, forever. Amen.'**

Thought for the day: Today I will look for signs of God's love and care.

Pallavi Sunit Macwan (Gujarat, India)

*Matthew 6:9–13 (KJV)

Unexpected opportunities

Read 2 Corinthians 9:6–15

God is able to bless you abundantly, so that in all things at all times, having all that you need, you will abound in every good work.
2 Corinthians 9:8 (NIV)

During a holiday trip, my daughter and her family stopped to eat at a takeaway restaurant. Because of a mix-up in their order, they ended up with an extra meal. As they headed back to the motorway, they saw a young man holding a sign that said, 'Hungry. Please help.' They stopped a short distance from him, and our daughter rolled down her window. Calling to him, she said, 'We have an extra meal if you would like it.' The young man gratefully took the food, smiled and then lifted the food and his eyes heavenward as if he were saying a quiet thank you. My daughter and her family felt a sense of gratitude for having been given the extra meal and for being in the right place at the right time to help meet a young man's need.

Reflecting on my daughter's story, I remember similar events in my own life – times when I've received something unexpected and then had an opportunity to use it to meet someone's need. Unfortunately, I have not always acted on the opportunity or simply haven't recognised it until it has passed.

Each day we can be aware of opportunities to make a difference in someone's life, and we can ask God for the courage to share our gifts and blessings.

Prayer: *Thank you, Father, for your many gifts and unexpected blessings. Help us to seek and to act on the opportunities you provide us to share with those in need. Amen*

Thought for the day: With whom will I share something in God's name today?

Byron S. Wills (Oregon, US)

PRAYER FOCUS: THOSE WITHOUT ENOUGH TO EAT

Praising God all day

Read 1 Thessalonians 5:16–18

[The Lord] is your praise; he is your God, who has done for you these great and awesome things that your own eyes have seen.
Deuteronomy 10:21 (NRSV)

After our grandson was born, I went to my son and daughter-in-law's house to help out. I was so caught up in taking care of the house and the baby that I realised I was not making time for my regular prayer and Bible reading. But then I realised I had been praying and rejoicing all the time! The feeling of awe I had as I gazed into my grandson's face was prayer. Each time I marvelled at my grandson's features and his ability to eat, move and coo, I was praising God and being thankful for his life, my life and the love that our family has for one another.

Observing God's gifts around me – the miracles of nature, the perfections of a newborn baby – expanded my ability to worship the creator. Each day now I try to find new blessings to be thankful for and to incorporate my praise into prayer.

The birth of my grandson and the overwhelming love I feel for this child have given me a sense of how strong God's love for us must be. Watching my son and daughter-in-law take on the responsibility of lovingly caring for the basic needs of their newborn child is just another reason to praise God and to know how much he loves us.

Prayer: *Gracious God, we thank you for families and for our ability to show love as you have shown love for us. In Jesus' name, we pray. Amen*

Thought for the day: I can praise God throughout the day, not just at devotion time.

Mary Ellen Piland (North Carolina, US)

True freedom

Read Galatians 5:13–18

It is for freedom that Christ has set us free. Stand firm, then, and do not let yourselves be burdened again by a yoke of slavery.
Galatians 5:1 (NIV)

When I was young, I had a dog named Ollie. He was tiny, but intelligent. When I rattled keys in my hand, he would spring to his feet and grab his lead with his mouth. Once we were outside, he would stay close to me as long as his lead remained in his mouth. When I took the lead from him, he knew he was free to run to his heart's content.

Some people are physically free, yet remain imprisoned by guilt, self-hatred or financial obligations. I am currently imprisoned on death row because of mistakes I made when I was a prisoner to gangs, money and drugs. But the apostle Paul tells us that 'it is for freedom that Christ has set us free'. Christ offers me a freedom that releases me spiritually from my cold, damp prison cell to live as a follower of his way.

When those in prison are released, they receive 'discharge papers' to let everyone know they are now free. Christ offers us all discharge papers. If we ask Jesus into our hearts, we receive the spiritual and mental freedom that comes only through him. I may never know physical freedom, but I have found joy, peace, love and a strong faith community. Christ can rattle the keys that signal real freedom for those who walk with him.

Prayer: *Dear God, as we rejoice in the freedom that you provide, help us also to comfort those who are imprisoned by the heavy burdens of life. In Jesus' name. Amen*

Thought for the day: No walls on earth can keep us from freedom in Christ.

Raymond Johnson (Oklahoma, US)

Anticipation

Read Psalm 130:5–8

I wait for the Lord more than watchmen wait for the morning.
Psalm 130:6 (NIV)

Over the course of 28 years of ministry, I've sat with hundreds of families in dozens of hospital waiting rooms. It's an agonising time filled with sorrow, loneliness and fear. Virtually every family tells me that waiting is the worst part. No one likes this kind of sad, passive waiting.

But another kind of waiting moves us to put up trees, light candles and hang wreaths. This anticipation brings joy. It thrills our souls. We look forward to it all year long – waiting for the appearance of the Christ child. As we mark each day off the calendar, the excitement grows, moving us to acts of love and kindness towards friends and strangers alike. We wait, full of hope, because we know that good news is coming to a manger and into our hearts. This Advent, may we join the psalmist in singing, 'I wait for the Lord more than watchmen wait for the morning.'

That sleepy guard on the last watch of the night stands in anticipation of the sunrise that will set him free from his toil. In a similar way, we wait this month with excitement for the appearance of the Son who will set us free.

Prayer: *Loving God, fill our lives with hope that moves us to acts of kindness. Amen*

Thought for the day: This Advent, I will wait in eager anticipation for the Lord.

Kevin L. Thomas (Alabama, US)

A wonderful blessing

Read Genesis 45:1–15

Do not be distressed and do not be angry with yourselves for selling me here, because it was to save lives that God sent me ahead of you.
Genesis 45:5 (NIV)

My family relies on me for help financially. While my friends go shopping for new clothes, bags or shoes, I must save money to pay the rent for my family's home. While my friends go on holiday, I have to save money for my father's medical care. I'm sometimes tempted to feel sorry for myself. I have days when I think my life is unfair. Then I remember Joseph. His brothers sold him into slavery in Egypt, but God raised him to a position of power and honour. Joseph recognised the responsibility that God gave him to save his family from severe famine. Rather than focusing on himself and how he could enjoy his privileged life, Joseph helped his family.

Joseph's story reminds me that it is important to bless others. Instead of sometimes dwelling on how unfortunate I feel, I thank God for the wonderful opportunity I have to be a blessing to my family.

Prayer: *God of grace, thank you for opportunities to be a blessing to others. Amen*

Thought for the day: I will joyfully accept opportunities to bless others today.

Linawati Santoso (East Java, Indonesia)

Unmerited favour

Read John 8:1–11

When they came to the place called the Skull, they crucified him there… Jesus said, 'Father, forgive them, for they do not know what they are doing.'
Luke 23:33–34 (NIV)

As I backed out of the driveway, my girlfriend, Misty, and I were chatting with our friends in the back seat. A horrible metallic shriek and intense jarring of the car silenced us all. I had just backed over a huge boulder beside the driveway that was meant to keep people from driving on the grass. The car belonged to Misty's parents. Her mother gaped from the kitchen window. Before we left, she had told us to be careful. Near tears and shamefaced, Misty and I entered the house to beg her mum's forgiveness. Instantly she said, 'I forgive you', handing us the keys to her other car. She then interrupted our protests to say, 'I said I forgive you. Now just be careful and have a good time.'

I wasn't yet a Christian, but that one act of forgiveness by a Christian is what helped me to believe in God's forgiveness, which I've had to ask for countless times since. And now, as a believer, it reminds me to be generous in forgiving others. Because God continues to forgive me when I get things wrong, and because a Christian modelled that same mercy towards me, I am now better able to forgive others.

Prayer: *Dear God, help us to forgive others in the same way that you have forgiven us. Amen*

Thought for the day: When I forgive someone, I am showing that person an image of Christ.

George T. Wilkerson (North Carolina, US)

Finding rest

Read 2 Samuel 15:13–26
I lie down and sleep; I wake again, because the Lord sustains me.
Psalm 3:5 (NIV)

While walking on the beach, my wife and I came across a very large green turtle lying by the water's edge. It lay motionless on the sand throughout the day, opening its eyes briefly only when someone went close to it. I wondered why it was there and what it was doing. Later we phoned a local marine observatory, and the staff told me that green turtles rest on the shore where they are safe from harm.

In 2 Samuel 15 we read of David's flight from Jerusalem. David did not know what the future held for him. Yet he was not consumed with fear and anxiety. He was content to leave the future in God's hands, a God who knows the end from the beginning. Like the turtle that was able to rest on the beach, David was able to rest because he knew that God's care and protection surrounded him. When our future seems uncertain and fear and anxiety overwhelm us, we too can lie down and rest, knowing that God is in control of all things.

Prayer: *Dear Lord, help us to trust in your mercy and grace. When our future looks uncertain, thank you for loving us and caring for us. Amen*

Thought for the day: Even in the midst of uncertainty, I can rest in God's presence.

Awlwyn Balnave (British Columbia, Canada)

Grandmother's kitchen

Read 1 Peter 4:8–11

Dear children, let us not love with words or speech but with actions and in truth.
1 John 3:18 (NIV)

My grandmother's kitchen was a special place; I still have warm memories of it. Grandmother didn't need any written recipes for her meals because she had memorised just how much of each ingredient to put in. And every meal was delicious. She was especially good at baking cakes, and every Christmas my friends and I would gather to get the first bite of cake fresh from the oven. When I asked her what her secret ingredient was – that special something that made her cooking taste so much better than anyone else's – she just smiled and said, 'The special ingredient is love.'

God gives each of us gifts, and we show his love for us when we put those gifts to work in the world around us. Learning the words of the Lord and then not putting action behind those words is like reading recipes and then not cooking anything. Just as my grandmother brightened the world around her, we can show God's love to others in such a way that whoever tastes what God offers will know that they have tasted the world's greatest love.

Prayer: *Dear God, you have given us gifts to do good. May we always use your teachings to help others. Amen*

Thought for the day: When I help others, I show God's love living in me.

Mark A. Carter (Oregon, US)

A little tweaking

Read Ephesians 1:15–23

I keep asking that the God of our Lord Jesus Christ, the glorious Father, may give you the Spirit of wisdom and revelation, so that you may know him better.
Ephesians 1:17 (NIV)

During my eye test, my optician said, 'I may tweak your prescription a little.' I hadn't noticed any problems with my eyesight, but I replied, 'Well, if a little tweak is going to improve my vision, that's good. Who wouldn't want that?'

I began to think about tweaking other areas of my life. I have often tweaked a recipe or a dressmaking pattern in the hope of making it a little better. What would happen if I tweaked my devotional time? I have a regular habit of meeting the Lord in the morning with two devotional booklets I use with my Bible, and I have been satisfied with that. Yet, a more deliberate Bible reading or prayer practice can make a difference. By reading slowly for deeper meaning, or by pausing to listen for God's answers, I might experience greater understanding.

I have found this greater understanding, as well as an increased desire for daily devotional time, after only moderate changes to my approach. Tweaking may be different for each person. Whatever the change – if we can draw closer to the Lord and hear him more clearly, who wouldn't want that?

Prayer: *Dear God, give us the desire to learn more about you each day. Amen*

Thought for the day: I will never finish learning about God.

Connie Cousins (Pennsylvania, US)

Hornets' nest

Read Galatians 3:23–29

Though he may stumble, he will not fall, for the Lord upholds him with his hand.
Psalm 37:24 (NIV)

When I was young, my brother and I used to visit our grandparents. They lived in a rural area near a narrow railway track. We used to walk down it and explore. One day, when I was six years old, I heard a strange sound and went over to a thicket of blackberry bushes to investigate. The sound was coming from a hornets' nest. In my panic to get away, I became trapped in the spiny blackberry bushes. My brother, who was twelve, rushed in and untangled me, ignoring all the stings he was getting. He freed me and took me to Grandma's house, where I was treated for the stings. When I had been cared for, we discovered that my brother had ended up with twice as many stings as I had and still had hornets in his jacket attacking his arms.

Though my earthly brother has since passed away, I am reminded that I still have a protector in Christ. Jesus freely went to his death to save us. And he still helps us whenever we get into a 'nest of hornets' that we can't seem to escape. Psalm 37:4 is God's promise and our hope for those blackberry-bush days.

Prayer: *Dear Lord, thank you for all the times that you have helped us through difficult situations. Help us to trust in your promise to uphold us when we stumble. Amen*

Thought for the day: I have a protector who will always rescue me.

Ken Claar (Idaho, US)

Power over fear

Read 2 Timothy 1:6–14

God hath not given us the spirit of fear; but of power, and of love, and of a sound mind.

2 Timothy 1:7 (KJV)

When I was young, I was afraid of going into our cellar. With only one dim light overhead, the cellar was eerie and dark with many shadows and corners. What made it even more dreadful was a huge octopus-like furnace with large tentacles coming out from the top of its head. When my dad opened the door to shovel coal into what looked like an angry pit, the fire and bright red coals inside the furnace looked like the entrance into another world, one that I greatly feared.

As I grew older, I realised that irrational fear like this – and the bad choices I might make as a result of it – could permeate my mind in such a subtle way that I am sometimes unaware of its influence.

Psalm 121 tells us that our help comes from God, who is by our side at all times. By God's power we can move forward, even in our fear.

Paul reminded Timothy to be bold in the face of adversity and that the power of the Holy Spirit was with him. So the next time we feel dread, we can ask God to give us the courage to move forward with power, love and a sound mind, calmed by God's Spirit.

Prayer: *Dear God, thank you for giving us strength in times of doubt. We know you are with us at all times. Give us a spirit of power and love, and dispel our fears. Amen*

Thought for the day: God's Spirit moves us forward in the face of adversity.

Terrye Blevins (Michigan, US)

Give thanks

Read Psalm 103:1–5
Give thanks in every situation because this is God's will for you in Christ Jesus.
1 Thessalonians 5:18 (CEB)

During a routine appointment with my cardiologist, I realised that, although I felt healthy, my physical condition was more precarious than I wanted to admit. He was amazed that I had survived so many health challenges, but following the appointment I felt scared and depressed.

After giving the situation more thought the next day, I decided to thank God for the good that would come through this difficulty. I gave thanks that my situation was teaching me the brevity of life and how important it is to do God's will (see Psalm 90:12). I also thanked God that I learned of another medical problem during the doctor's appointment so that I can manage the issue before it becomes serious.

I find it easy to thank God when life feels good but difficult when I'm afraid. Yet we can find something to be thankful for in all situations. We can trust God's promise to bring good from the circumstances that cause us to fear. As Paul wrote, 'We know that God works all things together for good for the ones who love God, for those who are called according to his purpose' (Romans 8:28).

Prayer: *Help us, Lord, to trust you to bring good things from any difficulty we face. Amen*

Thought for the day: I will give thanks to God in every situation.

Richard Kehoe (California, US)

Praying for guidance

Read Philippians 4:4–9

Do not worry about anything, but in everything by prayer and supplication with thanksgiving let your requests be made known to God.

Philippians 4:6 (NRSV)

When I left high school, I did not know what to do. Since 2016, I had been looking for a college athletic scholarship in the United States, but I had difficulties with the entrance exams that I needed to take. Many people told me that they thought I couldn't pass the exams and go to the United States to pursue my goal.

By the summer of 2017, most of my classmates knew what college they would attend, but I didn't. Everyone asked me what I was going to do, and when I told them that I was going to the States they still told me that I couldn't do it. Time passed, and I still did not have a college to attend. My parents were worried, and my dad thought that I would never make it; he was about to send me to a university in Veracruz, but I refused.

Eventually I stopped believing in myself, so I started talking to God for guidance through the process. I was reminded of Philippians 4:6, which says, 'Do not worry about anything.' In the autumn of 2017, I received an email telling me that I had been accepted to an American college. I know that I will never be alone because God is with me.

Prayer: *Thank you, Lord, for helping us through our problems and for never abandoning us. Amen*

Thought for the day: Even when I don't believe in myself, God believes in me.

Adriana Carpenter del Rivero (Veracruz, Mexico)

All are invited

Read Matthew 22:1–10
Go to the street corners and invite to the banquet anyone you find.
Matthew 22:9 (NIV)

Ellis Anne, our six-year-old granddaughter, was being taught by her parents that her classmates' birthday parties are by invitation and require parental approval. When my wife and I made our 260-mile trip to visit, Ellis Anne greeted us with the question, 'Were you invited?' My wife explained that we were invited, and that we are family.

The gospels tell us that Jesus was often invited to the homes of others for meals, weddings and parties, and to visit the sick and dying. Many of his parables are about invitations to banquets and parties. The gospel of Luke is full of examples, and we also see banquets in the story of the last supper and the post-resurrection meals in the gospel of John.

When we look at the gospels and think about Ellis Anne's question, we can see that *everyone* is invited to come to God's table. That is the good news. All are God's children, and he wants us all to come to the banquet – life in fellowship with all his children and his creation. As servants of God, we have the privilege and the commission to invite everyone to come and share in fellowship as his family.

Prayer: *Dear God, help us to share your love through our words and deeds. May we show all your children that they are invited to live in fellowship. Amen*

Thought for the day: All people are children of God, and all are invited.

John Sawyer (South Carolina, US)

God waits

Read Psalm 63:1–8

God gives wisdom, knowledge, and joy to those who please God.
Ecclesiastes 2:26 (CEB)

During prayer time at our church one morning, our minister asked us to hold hands with those beside us. Cole, my very energetic two-year-old son, was quietly playing with his toy tractor when I reached out my hand to hold his. He held my hand for a second, but shortly afterwards went back to running his toy up and down the pew. A short while later the tractor was in my waiting hand, broken into two pieces but fixable. I put it back together for him and continued to hold out my hand. He took the toy, then grasped my hand for a while.

During all of this, I started thinking how God always keeps a hand out waiting for us, even when we're happily going on with our life ignoring him or not putting him first. Despite this, when we go to God with our life that has broken into pieces, he puts us back together. We then have a choice to thank him and to take hold of his hand, or to go back to ignoring him. Either way, God waits for us. Praise be to God for his ever-beckoning hand and his unconditional love.

Prayer: *Dear God, forgive us for the times we ignore you. Thank you for always being there to put us back together and to provide true contentment and meaning for our lives. Amen*

Thought for the day: God is always waiting, eager to mend us.

Stacey Phillips (Virginia, US)

Jimmy joined up

Read Matthew 4:18–22
'Come, follow me,' Jesus said.
Matthew 4:19 (NIV)

A special service was held in the church to celebrate the 80th anniversary of the founding of the Boys' Brigade company. The minister welcomed everyone, including the boys, their parents, church members and earlier members of the Boys' Brigade. He concluded his welcome by saying that it was highly unlikely that any of the first members would be present at the service. How wrong he was.

One evening, back in 1935, nine-year-old Jimmy was playing football in the local park. Word went round that the church was about to start up a Boys' Brigade company, and names were being taken that very night. Jimmy and two of his friends ran up to the church hall and enlisted there and then.

Jimmy progressed through the ranks of the company and became a lieutenant. He might have become the company captain but when he married he and his wife joined a different church nearer to where they lived. He served there as a member and elder for many years, but he was still keen to attend the anniversary of his old company. At the end of the service Jimmy slipped away quietly to visit his wife in hospital. She, like Jimmy, is a lifelong follower of the Lord.

Prayer: *Dear Lord, we thank you for calling us to follow you. Help us to serve you faithfully all our days. Amen*

Thought for the day: Today I will look for ways to serve the Lord.

William Findlay (Glasgow, Scotland)

Bearing fruit

Read John 15:1–8

[Jesus said,] 'I am the vine; you are the branches. If you remain in me and I in you, you will bear much fruit; apart from me you can do nothing.'
John 15:5 (NIV)

A few weeks ago, my minister preached about the fruitful tree of John 15. 'Even when the tree bears much fruit, it never enjoys any of it,' he said. 'The fruit is produced to be enjoyed by other living things, human or animal, that eat from the tree.' I really like fruit, especially grapes, melons, apples and oranges. But after hearing this sermon, whenever I eat fruit, I remember the fruitful tree and savour the taste even more.

In a similar way, God wants our lives to bear much fruit so we can be a blessing to others. To be fruitful, we must always remain in Jesus. 'Remain in me,' he said, 'as I also remain in you. No branch can bear fruit by itself; it must remain in the vine. Neither can you bear fruit unless you remain in me' (John 15:4).

We remain in Jesus by reading and meditating on God's word each day and putting it into practice. When we bear much fruit, we can be a blessing to others. When we become a blessing to others, we bring glory to God.

Prayer: *Dear God, help us to remain in you and your love so that we can bear much fruit. May we be a blessing to others and glorify your name. Amen*

Thought for the day: I can glorify God by being a blessing to others.

Meliana Santoso (East Java, Indonesia)

Healing

Read Psalm 118:1–14

The Lord is my strength and my defence; he has become my salvation.
Psalm 118:14 (NIV)

The December flight home was late, long and lonely as I grieved the unexpected loss of my brother. Forty-one was too young to die. I prayed for strength to face his funeral and a Christmas without him. I had yet to post Christmas cards or finish my shopping. I had not decorated the house or prepared any treats for the grandchildren. I just wanted to go home and crawl under the covers – maybe forever.

After midnight, I finally arrived home. I looked around in wonder. My daughter and her family had paid a visit. They left a sparkling clean house, a small lighted tree and, best of all, put out our family nativity scene. The heart of all our holiday traditions, it stood in its usual place of honour – complete with the stable my husband had made nearly 35 years earlier. Every figure was there. As I knelt, cradling the baby Jesus figurine in my hands, I felt as if Christ himself were cradling me in his arms. Tears of hope flowed down my cheeks. I knew that painful days of grief still awaited me but also that my brother was standing in God's presence. I would see him again.

Even when grief replaces the cards, chocolate, tinsel and presents, Christmas remains. For Christmas is the Christ who 'is my strength and my defence… my salvation'.

Prayer: *Abba Father, thank you for the gift of your Son, for your comfort in loss and the hope of heaven. In Jesus' name. Amen*

Thought for the day: I can comfort others as God has comforted me.

Rhonda K. Maller (Indiana, US)

PRAYER FOCUS: GRATITUDE FOR SOMEONE WHO HAS HELPED ME

A blank canvas

Read Galatians 5:22–26

The fruit of the Spirit is love, joy, peace, forbearance, kindness, goodness, faithfulness, gentleness and self-control.
Galatians 5:22–23 (NIV)

Many years ago I took an open-air landscape painting class using oil paints. I loved the idea of painting landscapes while surrounded by nature, but I was not very good at it. Fortunately, oil paints take a while to dry; so when you mess up the picture you simply wipe the paint off the canvas with a knife and start again!

I imagine God's hand in my life the same way. I start each day with a blank canvas. The colours that appear on my canvas can be from the fruit of the Spirit – love, joy, peace, forbearance, kindness, goodness, faithfulness, gentleness and self-control. Or they can be from my prideful self – my judgement, negativity, selfishness. I see the colours of the Spirit as bright yellows, oranges, blues and greens, and the colours of pride as drab and grey.

At the end of the day, if I find that my canvas is full of drab and grey colours, God wipes it clean. Then I can start a new day with a blank canvas so that he can paint the vibrant colours of the fruit of the Spirit and begin a masterpiece in me.

Prayer: *Lord, give us wisdom to know that you are always here with your grace to forgive our sins. May we know that we are always welcome in your presence. Amen*

Thought for the day: What colours will appear on the canvas that God has given me today?

Kendra Lelie (Pennsylvania, US)

God's surprises

Read Luke 1:26–38

The angel went to [Mary] and said, 'Greetings, you who are highly favoured! The Lord is with you.' Mary was greatly troubled at his words and wondered what kind of greeting this might be.
Luke 1:28–29 (NIV)

A week before Christmas we arrived at the airport to go home. During the previous eleven days, my husband and I had spent many long hours helping people with the clear-up after tornadoes had torn through the area. We were exhausted and left with little time to prepare to celebrate Jesus' birth.

As we entered the airport, we heard a children's choir singing familiar Christmas carols. I was moved to tears. In an unlikely place, God surprised us with those lovely voices. My preparation for Christmas had begun.

God is full of surprises in the Christmas story. Mary was startled by the visit of Gabriel. Joseph was surprised by his visit from an angel (Matthew 1:18–25). All except the religious scholars were surprised that the Christ child would be born in Bethlehem (Matthew 2:4–5).

We too can be surprised by God. If we look, we may see him in the expectant eyes of a child or the desperate look in the face of someone who is homeless or hungry. We can bring God's presence into the emptiness where relationships are broken or into the loneliness in families grieving the death of a loved one. During Advent, we can look beyond our busyness to see God in unexpected places.

Prayer: *Dear God, give us eyes to see, ears to hear and minds to recognise your presence in the midst of our hectic lives. Amen*

Thought for the day: Today I will look for God in unlikely places.

Cherri Baer (Kansas, US)

Overcoming darkness

Read John 1:1–14

The light shines in the darkness, and the darkness has not overcome it.

John 1:5 (NIV)

When my phone rang at 6.00 am on that Sunday morning, it was my wife calling with news that her father had died. In my sorrow, I realised that I needed to plan for others to assume my responsibilities at church, inform our children of their grandfather's death and prepare for the 700-mile trip to be with my family for his funeral.

As I walked from our house to the church, the sky was still dark, as dark and despairing as I felt. Suddenly I looked up and saw a large lighted star atop the tallest building in our town. I'm sure it had been there other mornings, but I'd never noticed. At this moment, it seemed to be saying, 'Look! Look at me! It's not as dark as you think.' I was filled with hope. I sensed 'Emmanuel' – God with us.

As we travel through Advent towards celebrating another Christmas, we may find ourselves walking in darkness – weary, grieving or burdened by health or financial issues or other concerns about the future. At such times, we can remember John's testimony about Jesus: 'The light shines in the darkness, and the darkness has not overcome it.'

Prayer: *God of light and love, help us to sense your nearness in these days. Be for us a light in the darkness of our lives. Amen*

Thought for the day: Christ's light dispels the darkness in my life.

Bob Baer (Kansas, US)

Surefooted

Read Psalm 1

Strengthen your feeble arms and weak knees. 'Make level paths for your feet,' so that the lame may not be disabled, but rather healed.
Hebrews 12:12–13 (NIV)

For several months my severe arthritis affected my gait. When I watched a video of myself walking, I was astonished. My right foot slanted, causing me to limp.

Seeing the way I walked made me think of the way that problems we face can cause us to drift away from our spiritual path. Trials tend to drain our physical and mental strength. However, when we take our questions and troubles to God through prayer and Bible study, we find our weak feet becoming sturdy and strong. As Habakkuk discovered, 'The Sovereign Lord is my strength; he makes my feet like the feet of a deer, he enables me to tread on the heights' (Habakkuk 3:19).

Sometimes when we think we are going smoothly along the spiritual path, we may boastfully take credit for our stable footing. At those times, we might want to heed the words of Isaiah: 'All of us have become like one who is unclean, and all our righteous acts are like filthy rags; we all shrivel up like a leaf, and like the wind our sins sweep us away' (Isaiah 64:6). It is God to whom we give the glory for providing us with strength and security.

Prayer: *Loving heavenly Father, help us to walk in your sure ways and clear path. In the name of our Lord and Saviour, Jesus Christ. Amen*

Thought for the day: God is a sure footing for my life.

Urvashi H. Parmar (Gujarat, India)

Jesus is here! Come and see!

Read Luke 2:8–20
This will be a sign to you: you will find a baby wrapped in cloths and lying in a manger.
Luke 2:12 (NIV)

The days leading up to Christmas are very exciting, especially when you have three small children. At our church a nativity scene was put out on the first Sunday in Advent. My two-year-old ran to look at it and peered inside the stable. He asked me why there was no baby and I said that the baby would not be added until Christmas Day. Each week he would run to look inside and sadly shake his head, saying, 'No baby. Not Christmas.'

On Christmas Day when we arrived at church he ran straight to the stable, looked inside and then turned round with the biggest beaming smile, shouting at the top of his voice: 'He's here! Jesus is really here! It's Christmas Day – come and see everyone!' The congregation left the church that morning praising God and talking of the little boy who had urged them to 'come and see' Jesus.

On that first Christmas morning the shepherds too ran to the stable to look and see that Jesus had come. The Saviour was born at last! They left praising and glorifying God. How important it is to remind ourselves that God came to earth as a baby born in a stable.

Prayer: *Lord, thank you for coming to earth as a baby, to show us how to live in love. Amen*

Thought for the day: Today I will urge others to 'come and see' Jesus.

Pam Lewis (Essex, England)

The longest journey

Read Psalm 86:1–13

Teach me to do your will, for you are my God. Let your good spirit lead me on a level path.
Psalm 143:10 (NRSV)

I have taken many journeys in my lifetime and travelled to many different places. I have marvelled at the time it took to carve out the Grand Canyon. I have stood on the shore and watched dolphins frolic in the waves. I have gone deep into caves and been in awe of great stalagmites, and I have flown above the patchwork of crop fields.

Some journeys are not measured in miles but in years. I was married for a quarter of a century until my wife died. I watched my children grow into adults. And I have been in prison for nearly ten years.

Yet my longest journey began when I accepted Jesus into my life. This trip changed me completely, and it will take the rest of my life. I will never travel alone on this journey, because the Holy Spirit is at my side and Jesus leads the way. A multitude of travellers accompany me on the same road and I'm grateful for all of them. The cost has been paid, my itinerary has been set and the route has been marked. In the distance I can see my glorious home.

Prayer: *Dear God, thank you for being with us on our journey and for the promise of a home with you in heaven when this life is over. In Jesus' name. Amen*

Thought for the day: Because Jesus is with me, I never have to travel alone.

Russell Tarver (Wyoming, US)

My calling

Read Mark 10:13–16

People were bringing little children to him in order that he might touch them.

Mark 10:13 (NRSV)

For over 45 years, I've cared for the needs of children – my children, friends' children, neighbourhood children, my grandchildren and my great-grandchildren. I've spent much of my life changing nappies, wiping runny noses, soothing hurts and reading storybooks.

I must admit that there have been times when I've questioned whether what I'm doing serves any purpose in God's kingdom. Does making cakes and painting pictures count for much? Does wiping away tears or simply being there for a child make a difference? But then I remember Jesus welcoming the little children and gathering them into his arms. Jesus said, 'It is to such as these [children] that the kingdom of God belongs.'

When I read this verse, I realise that what I do is important. This is my calling – to be there for children, greet them at the door, play with them, pray for them and tell them about Jesus. Caring for children provides opportunities to show them through our words and actions how much Jesus loves them.

Prayer: *Thank you, God, for allowing us to be witnesses of your love. Help us to grow closer to you each day. Amen*

Thought for the day: Today I will look for Jesus in the face of every child.

Linda Knight (Ontario, Canada)

Large and small

Read Psalm 56:3–11

Trust in the Lord with all your heart and lean not on your own understanding; in all your ways submit to him, and he will make your paths straight.
Proverbs 3:5–6 (NIV)

Recently at the Christian foodbank where I help, we held hands in prayer for a fellow volunteer who was about to begin a strenuous series of surgical procedures to help alleviate some of his symptoms of Parkinson's disease. Our prayer was for healing, but more importantly, we asked for God's will to be done as well as for comfort for him, his wife and his family. Cliff, who was leading the prayer, said something that made a deep impression on me: 'God, we trust you with our salvation and our eternity; surely we can trust you with this.'

How often do I worry that God is not going to handle the situation or sort out the problem? How often do I not even take it to the Lord, wanting to address the problem on my own? Our Bible verse today says to submit all to the Lord, who will direct our life. God can handle all situations – large and small. If I trust God to take care of my eternal life, how can I possibly not trust him to take care of all the smaller things in my life too?

Prayer: *Dear God, thank you for caring for us in each and every situation. Help us to accept your care with gratitude and to put our trust in you. Amen*

Thought for the day: I can trust God today and always.

James C. Leyrer (Ohio, US)

To be a giver again

Read 2 Corinthians 8:1–5

[The Macedonian churches] urgently pleaded with us for the privilege of sharing in this service to the Lord's people.
2 Corinthians 8:4 (NIV)

For months people had been giving to me while I struggled with cancer. But it was hard to be in a Christmas mood when I had nothing to give others – no gifts, not even my time. I felt useless and angry. I was used to being a giver, not a taker.

I decided to go see a Christmas show, hoping it would get me into the Christmas spirit. During the interval, I won a voucher for a Christian summer camp for teenagers. It was as useless to me as I felt to the rest of the world. As the usher handed me the voucher, I suddenly felt the need to turn around. Behind me sat a mother speaking to her teenage daughter about the camp prize. 'Don't give up. Look how close you came to winning,' the mother said, pointing at me.

'Merry Christmas!' I said, handing over the prize. Tears ran down both their faces, and the daughter thanked me repeatedly. It turned out that for years she had prayed to attend a Christian summer camp. I had also prayed to be a giver again. What a sign of God's greatness and love! That night, I went home and put up some Christmas lights while the spirit of Christmas shone brightly within me.

Prayer: *Thank you, God, for answering prayer and providing us with opportunities to give to others. Amen*

Thought for the day: No matter what my circumstances are, God can always use me.

Nina Ward (Florida, US)

The great connection

Read Luke 2:1–14

An angel of the Lord appeared to [the shepherds], and the glory of the Lord shone around them.

Luke 2:9 (NIV)

As the Lord's angel appeared to the shepherds, God's presence brought brightness to that place. The angel told the good news to all people: the birth of the Saviour. While the angel was still delivering the message, a whole group of angels suddenly appeared – praising God, and saying: 'Glory to God in the highest heaven, and on earth peace to those on whom his favour rests' (Luke 2:14).

The angel's appearance to the shepherds reflects the bond we see embodied in the Christ child: the connection between heaven and earth, God and humans. God wants to have a relationship with each of us. Just as his presence brought brightness to the shepherds, he wants to brighten the lives of us all. In the midst of the challenges of life, God sends a message of joy through his Son, Jesus Christ. God loves us and on this and every Christmas Day he grants us lives full of peace.

Prayer: *Thank you, God, for sending us your Son, Jesus Christ, to shine his light in our lives and show us the path to salvation. In Jesus' name. Amen*

Thought for the day: God wants to shine his light into my life.

Wagner Oliveira dos Santos (Sao Paulo, Brazil)

Family history

Read Matthew 1:1–17

There were fourteen generations in all from Abraham to David, fourteen from David to the exile in Babylon, and fourteen from the exile to the Messiah.
Matthew 1:17 (NIV)

When I open up the first chapter of Matthew and read 17 verses of names, my first question is, 'Why?'

I think Matthew put the genealogy in for several reasons. Firstly, Jesus was human. We focus on Jesus as God quite often, but it's important to remember that he was also a man.

Secondly, several names on the list fulfil messianic prophecy. In Jeremiah 23:5, God says, 'I will raise up for David a righteous Branch, a King who will reign wisely.' Matthew wants to show that Jesus fulfilled that prophecy and many others.

Thirdly, this list proves that God can use anyone for divine purposes. On the list are Abraham, Ruth and David, heroes of the faith. But Rahab and Tamar were involved in prostitution, and Manasseh and Abijah didn't have the best reputations.

Jesus' family tree included all kinds, more than a few who were disreputable. But God worked through all of them.

Sometimes, we may wonder how God could possibly work through us. Matthew reminds us that God can and does work through each and every one of us.

Prayer: *Dear God, help us to see how you are working through the people around us. Open our hearts to serve you each day. Amen*

Thought for the day: How is God working through me?

Hannah Meyer (California, US)

God is good

Read Psalm 119:65–72

You are good, and what you do is good.
Psalm 119:68 (NIV)

I spent Christmas Day with my dad at the hospital. At times, I heard groans from other patients. When I heard them, I whispered a prayer for them. This was a difficult time, but it had a purpose. The psalmist wrote, 'It was good for me to be afflicted so that I might learn your decrees' (v. 71). Difficult times help us to rely more on God.

When we face challenges, we can still find peace and hope. Even in difficult times, we can trust in God's ways because God is good, and we can trust that he is working out what is best for us and drawing us closer. Like the psalmist, we can be assured of God's goodness and say, 'You have treated your servant well, Lord, according to your promise' (v. 65, CEB). Thanks be to God.

Prayer: *Dear God, help us to see your goodness even as we go through difficult times. As Jesus taught us, we pray, 'Our Father in heaven, hallowed be your name, your kingdom come, your will be done, on earth as it is in heaven. Give us today our daily bread. Forgive us our debts, as we also have forgiven our debtors. And lead us not into temptation, but deliver us from the evil one.'* Amen*

Thought for the day: God always wants the best for me.

Mary Ng Shwu Ling (Singapore)

No burden too heavy

Read Mark 16:1–8

[The women] were saying to each other, 'Who's going to roll the stone away from the entrance for us?'
Mark 16:3 (CEB)

While chasing a ball that my grandson threw, I tripped and fell face down on my drive. The crunching noise of my teeth against the concrete and the gushing blood from my mouth and nose were frightening. As a surgeon, my biggest fears were that I had a skull fracture or bleeding in the brain. An ambulance took me to hospital, and thankfully the scan of my head showed no fracture or bleeding inside the skull. My worries were unfounded.

Following this incident, I could identify with the women on their way to the tomb on the first Easter Sunday. They had been worried about the huge stone at the entrance, not knowing that God had already moved it for them. Life throws different types of 'stones' on our paths. When we are faced with problems that are too much for us to handle, we can turn to God. No burden is too heavy for him to carry and no stone too large for him to move – he is willing and able to sustain us through any trial or suffering.

Prayer: *Dear God, thank you for moving the heavy stones from our paths. Help us to trust you through our trials. Amen*

Thought for the day: God is with me through frightening times.

K. E. Mathew (Louisiana, US)

God's helpers

Read Psalm 30:8–12

Be strong and courageous. Do not be afraid or terrified because of them, for the Lord your God goes with you; he will never leave you nor forsake you.
Deuteronomy 31:6 (NIV)

Sent by my Russian church to a Christian conference, I was travelling to Budapest. Many worries occupied me: I had no idea how to find the conference location; I couldn't afford a taxi; and I did not speak Hungarian. Among the passengers was an elderly Hungarian man who could help me, but I did not want to ask him. I thought that, like many of his generation, he might still remember the way the Russian Army crushed the Hungarian Revolution in 1956. So I was afraid that he would rebuff me. Finally, after a lengthy prayer, I approached him and presented my problem.

To my surprise he took my suitcase, accompanied me to the bus stop, bought my ticket and asked the driver to tell me where to get out. I tried to reimburse him, but he refused. He shook my hand, smiled at me and left.

On my way through Budapest's beautiful streets, I prayed and thanked my heavenly Father for sending me this helper. In the actions of this kind stranger, I saw the fulfilment of God's words: 'Never will I leave you; never will I forsake you' (Hebrews 13:5).

Prayer: *Dear Lord, help us to set aside our worry and instead trust you to be our refuge and strength. In Jesus' name. Amen*

Thought for the day: I will look for God's helper in all circumstances.

Tatiana Claudy (Indiana, US)

Not by our merits

Read Ephesians 2:4–9

By grace you have been saved, through faith – and this is not from yourselves, it is the gift of God – not by works, so that no one can boast.
Ephesians 2:8–9 (NIV)

Surrounded by overachievers my whole life, I've always felt that intelligence and talent are not my strongest characteristics. I feel pretty average most of the time. I was once again reminded of this at a pre-Christmas event at my church, where my friends were creating beautiful and intricately designed gingerbread houses, and I instead spent a few hours managing to create three alien-dog-looking reindeer.

Despite all this, and amid all my mediocrity, I have found peace in knowing the real beauty of Christmas: Jesus was born human, died on the cross to save us from our sins and rose to conquer death so that we may have eternal life.

In the verse quoted above, Paul assures us that our salvation doesn't depend on what we do or how mediocre we are but on what Jesus finished on the cross. As New Year's Day approaches and we remember all the resolutions we didn't fulfil last year, we can also take time to reflect on the limitations of relying on our own strength. Instead, we can rest in the real beauty of Christmas and the hope that Jesus offers.

Prayer: *Dear God, thank you for the peace we have in knowing that we can rest in your grace instead of our own merit. Amen*

Thought for the day: With God, I never have to rely on my strength alone.

Melissa Ramoo (New South Wales, Australia)

Beauty in the storm

Read Psalm 29
What manner of man is this, that even the winds and the sea obey him!
Matthew 8:27 (KJV)

One morning I stood praying in the empty sanctuary of my little church. As I looked out of the window at the changing weather, I could see that a cold front was moving in as dark, heavy clouds pushed across the sky. Though I was thankful to be sheltered inside, I also appreciated the beauty of the scene.

My thoughts turned to Psalm 29, where the glory of the Lord is found in the storm. Other scripture passages also talk about God amid the violence of the storm: in Nahum 1 the prophet thunders vengeance against sinful Nineveh. He uses the storm metaphors to describe the intense power of God's judgement. Yet right in the middle of the fury is a verse that stands out because of its incongruity. Verse 7 reads, 'The Lord is good, a strong hold in the day of trouble; and he knoweth them that trust in him' (KJV). What beauty amid the storm!

Finally, I thought of Jesus as he commanded the pounding rain, fierce waves and raging wind to be still. It made those around him recoil in awe: 'What manner of man is this!' No matter how ferocious the storm, God, who is beautiful, is in the midst of it. He is ever near to us – our shelter, our stronghold and our beautiful peace.

Prayer: *Dear God, thank you for being by our side during the storms of life. Amen*

Thought for the day: Even in the storm, I'm in the hands of God.

Rick Alexander (Virginia, US)

PRAYER FOCUS: VICTIMS OF NATURAL DISASTERS

Small group questions

Wednesday 4 September

1 Have you ever felt as if you were like the apple in today's meditation – lovely on the outside but not on the inside? What scripture verses encourage you when you feel this way?

2 What does it mean that Jesus Christ fights our battles with us? Describe a time when you experienced temptation and felt Christ's presence alongside you.

3 Does your church encourage you to persevere in the struggle between the good you want to do and the evil you do not want to do? What does your church do if someone is struggling with temptation?

4 What spiritual practices help you guard your heart from temptation?

5 Have you found that it gets easier to resist temptation and sin the longer you are a Christian? Or, like today's writer, do you find that no matter how long you've been a Christian you still struggle? Why do you think this is the case?

Wednesday 11 September

1 When have you wanted to pray but couldn't find the right words? What did you do? How do you pray in times like these?

2 How do you experience community with other Christians? During a crisis, do you find comfort in being with others who share your faith? As Christians, how can we help one another during difficult times?

3 What scripture passages give you a clear sense of what the early church looked like? What do you appreciate most about the early church?

4 What role does your church play in how you process tragedy?

5 What similarities do you see between your church today and the early church? Where do you see differences? How does your church help you in your faith journey?

Wednesday 18 September

1 Describe a time when you felt lonely. How did you respond to those feelings? What did you do to feel less lonely?

2 Have you ever felt called to serve but unsure of where to start? What did you do? Were there people in your life who helped you find ways to follow God's calling? How did they help you?

3 Does your church have outreach programmes to serve those in your community? Do you participate in them? If so, how does serving in this way enrich your life? If not, in what other ways do you serve your church and community?

4 When have you felt God's comfort? Did this encourage you to share that same comfort with others? What did you do?

5 Many biblical figures felt unsure of how to follow God's calling to serve. Which of these people do you most relate to? Why?

Wednesday 25 September

1 Who in your life reminds you that God is with you in difficult times? How do they help you remember that God will always be with you?

2 Describe a time when you wondered if God was still watching over you. What was the outcome of the situation? How did you deal with your doubts?

3 Jeremiah 29:11 brought today's writer and his family great comfort during their trials. Which verses comfort you during challenging situations?

4 What do you pray for when you are feeling hopeless? What spiritual practices strengthen your faith when you are going through trials?

5 Do you know someone who is going through a trial at the moment? How can you help and encourage this person? In what ways can you remind them that God still cares for them?

Wednesday 2 October

1 Describe a time when you asked God for guidance. Did his response bring you comfort? If so, how? If not, why not?

2 When you look back at your life's journey, do you see God walking with you? Where have you seen his presence and guidance most clearly?

3 How do you draw closer to God when you feel isolated? Do you find it easier to turn to him when you feel alone or when you are surrounded by others? When is your relationship with God the strongest?

4 Have you ever received an answer to prayer that was similar to the one in today's meditation? Do you appreciate more direct guidance from God? If so, why? Would it comfort you to have reassurance that God will be with you whatever you choose?

5 How do you reach out to those who are isolated? Does your church provide opportunities to develop a sense of community? In what ways do you try to connect with others?

Wednesday 9 October

1 Do you think of investing primarily in financial terms, like today's writer used to, or in spiritual terms? What does it mean to you to think about investing in your spiritual life?

2 How do you invest in spending time with God? How do you invest in your relationships with and service to others? What can you do to strengthen these relationships?

3 Today's writer says, 'Only God can evaluate our actions and judge the return on our investment.' Do you ever find yourself concerned with how others view your actions, rather than remembering that God's evaluation is most important? How do you deal with these feelings?

4 What things in your life distract you from focusing on God? What spiritual practices help you to prioritise your faith?

5 What does it look like to invest in your community? How can your church help you? How can you better serve others?

Wednesday 16 October

1 What barriers do you recognise in your life? Do you think you have other barriers that you are unaware of? What can you do to recognise these barriers?

2 What 'full freedom and blessings' does God want us to enjoy? How do we miss out on these things because of the invisible barriers in our lives?

3 Describe a time when you thought that you knew your motives for something you did, only to realise later that you didn't fully understand them. What did this experience teach you about yourself? What did it teach you about the role God plays in your understanding of yourself?

4 Today's writer suggests that we pray as David did in Psalm 139. Name your favourite prayers from scripture. What spiritual practices help you to better understand your heart?

5 Where do you recognise invisible barriers in your church? In your community? In the world? What do you think we can do to help expose these barriers and tear them down?

Wednesday 23 October

1 Do you have multiple roles that you fill? What roles do you not enjoy as much as others? What do you do when you don't feel like fulfilling one of your roles?

2 Do you struggle with wearing your faith outwardly every day? If not, what helps you avoid this struggle? If so, why? In what situations is it easiest for you to display your faith?

3 How can you better reflect your faith through your actions? What do you do when you feel that you are not reflecting your faith in the way you would like?

4 If you find yourself struggling to wear your faith proudly, how does your church community encourage you? What could you do to help another member of the congregation who is struggling in this way?

5 How do you ask God to restore your strength and help you display your faith to others? How does it encourage you to know that even if we hide our faith, God will help us show it through our actions?

Wednesday 30 October

1 Describe a time when you felt your faith was not big enough or strong enough to do what you hoped. What encouraged you during this time? Is it okay not to have 'huge' faith all the time? Why or why not?

2 Have you ever felt desperate for God to do something in your life or the life of someone you know? Did the situation turn out as you had hoped? What did this experience teach you about God's power and will for us?

3 Who in your life serves as an example of faith? What do you admire about this person's faith? Do you hope to serve as an example of faith for others? How will you do this?

4 What scripture passages bring you comfort when you feel your faith is not big enough?

5 Today's meditation talks about the bleeding woman from Mark 5. What other biblical figures come to mind when you think of a person's faith and God's power?

Wednesday 6 November

1 Describe a time when you had 'spiritual myopia'. At what point did you begin to see things more clearly? What helped you to do this?

2 Name a person in scripture who experienced 'spiritual myopia'. What can we learn from this person? What would you have done differently had you been in their shoes?

3 Whom do you find it difficult to treat with love and respect? Is it one person or a certain group of people? Why is it difficult for you? How can you begin to look on this person or group of people with the love and compassion of Jesus?

4 The writer of today's meditation says, 'We are called to witness to all people… regardless of their condition.' When has someone's 'condition' kept you from witnessing to them? Talk about this experience and what you learned from it.

5 How can you show more love and mercy to those in your community? Name three specific ways that you will show love and mercy to those around you this week.

Wednesday 13 November

1 Would you describe yourself as an anxious person? If so, how do you cope with your anxiety? If not, what prevents you from becoming anxious in situations that other people might find worrying?

2 What objects or practices remind you to give your worries to God? What spiritual disciplines do you practise in times of worry, frustration or doubt?

3 When have you fretted over the outcome of a situation? What happened? Did your worst fears come to pass? What were your prayers like during this time?

4 Do you find that it is easy or difficult to let go and give your worries to God? If your answer is 'easy', how so? If you responded with 'difficult', why is it hard?

5 What are you having trouble letting go of today? What would it look like for you to find peace in the situation? What outcome are you praying for? How can your church community support you through this?

Wednesday 20 November

1 Name someone from scripture who missed one of God's blessings that was right in front of them. What caused them to overlook the blessing? What do you think this story teaches us about God's blessings?

2 Have you ever discovered that you overlooked a blessing at some point in your life? How did it make you feel when you realised that you had missed it? Did it change the way that you look for God's blessings around you? If so, how?

3 In what ways can someone's past prevent them from moving forward? Why is it sometimes so hard not to dwell on the past? What helps you focus on the present and future?

4 What do you hope God has in store for your future? What do you hope God has in store for your community, your country and the world?

5 In the week ahead, try to be deliberate about noticing God's blessings around you. At the end of the week, reflect on which of these blessings you might have missed had you not been actively looking for them.

Wednesday 27 November

1 Describe a time when God has cared either for you or for someone you know in a miraculous way. What did this experience teach you about God's care and protection?

2 The 'Thought for the day' says, 'Today I will look for signs of God's love and care.' Where have you already noticed signs of God's love and care today?

3 When have you prayed about a situation that did not turn out as you had hoped? Did this change the way you think and feel about prayer? If so, how? If not, why not?

4 What spiritual practices do you engage in with family and/or friends? How have these practices shaped your spiritual journey? What advantages are there to praying and studying the Bible within a group?

5 Make a list of people in your church community who are going through a difficult time. In the coming week, commit to saying a prayer for each of these people every day. For what in the week ahead would you like the prayers of your church community?

Wednesday 4 December

1 When has your future seemed uncertain? What was your relationship with God like during this time in your life? Was it easy or challenging to trust God?

2 What does it mean to you to 'rest in God's presence'? Name practices that help you rest in God's presence. Who in scripture are good examples of resting in God's presence? What can we learn from them?

3 What is the most frightening situation that you have ever been in? How did you cope with your fear? Were you to ever find yourself in a similar situation again, what would you do differently?

4 Psalm 46:10 (NIV) says, 'Be still, and know that I am God.' What comfort and assurance does this verse give you? In what ways does it challenge you? What invitation does it offer?

5 Do you ever struggle to trust God? Why can trusting him sometimes be hard? What words of assurance would you offer to someone struggling to trust God today?

Wednesday 11 December

1 Suppose you were to host a party in your home. Whom would you be reluctant to invite? Why? What would make inviting this person less of a challenge?

2 When have you not received an invitation to an event to which you expected to be invited? How did it make you feel to be excluded?

3 What does it look like to be 'in fellowship with all of [God's] children and his creation'? What difficulties might this present? What opportunities?

4 How does your church community make people feel welcome and included? In what ways could it do a better job?

5 Name some stories from the gospels in which Jesus made people feel welcome. What can we learn from these stories? Is there ever a time when it is okay to exclude others? If so, when? If not, why not?

Wednesday 18 December

1 When have you found yourself 'walking in darkness – weary, grieving or burdened by health or financial issues'? What kept you close to God during this time in your life?

2 When have you been surprised by finding God's presence in a bleak situation? Why did it surprise you? What did it help you understand about God?

3 Is there ever a situation too hopeless for God's presence? Why or why not? Support your answer with examples from scripture.

4 Where are you praying for Christ's light to shine today? How can you help shine Christ's light in these places?

5 What volunteer opportunities exist in your community that you can take up during the Christmas season?

Wednesday 25 December

1 Which part of the nativity story is your favourite? Why? With whom in the story do you identify the most? With whom do you identify the least?

2 What special practices or observances do you participate in during the Christmas season? Which of these do you find most meaningful? Why?

3 In what ways has God brightened your life in the past year? In what ways do you hope that he will brighten your life in the year to come?

4 What evidence do you see in your life and in the lives of those around you that God wants to have a relationship with us? What can we do to make it easier for God to do so?

5 Spend a few moments in quiet reflection, considering what you are most thankful for today. Reflect on where you sense God's presence the most in your life. What new opportunities or invitation is God offering you?

Journal page

Journal page

As we look towards celebrating the incarnation at Christmas, we consider how God chose to express himself, in a moment in history, as a tiny baby. But what other images describe God in the Bible, and what can we learn about his character through them? How does an invisible God reveal himself to us in scripture and in Jesus? Amy Scott Robinson, a poet and storyteller, answers this question with imagination and a close reading of the text.

Image of the Invisible
Daily Bible readings from Advent to Epiphany
Amy Scott Robinson
978 0 85746 789 8   £8.99
brfonline.org.uk

The Rule of St Benedict has much to say about faith, work and daily living. In a time when many are seeking space, silence and spiritual depth, the Rule retains relevance in a world where change is often feared, stability can be elusive and busyness interferes with listening to God. *Life with St Benedict* provides daily reflections on the Rule as an aid to enabling personal spiritual growth and prayer.

Life with St Benedict
The Rule reimagined for everyday living
Richard Frost
978 0 85746 813 0 £9.99
brfonline.org.uk

A Fruitful Life
Abiding in Christ as seen in John 15

Tony Horsfall
Foreword by Steve Brady

In *A Fruitful Life* we ponder the teaching of Jesus in John 15, the famous 'vine' passage. Jesus is preparing his disciples for his departure and describing how they can be effective witnesses in a hostile world. Just as his instructions revolutionised their lives, so a proper understanding of what he is saying can revolutionise our lives also. It is the heart of the gospel message: the only way to live the Christian life is to allow Jesus to live his life in us and through us. This book includes material for individual reflection and questions for group discussion.

A Fruitful Life (second edition)
Abiding in Christ as seen in John 15
Tony Horsfall
978 0 85746 884 0 £8.99
brfonline.org.uk

Really Useful Guides

Each Really Useful Guide focuses on a specific biblical book, making it come to life for the reader, enabling them to understand the message and to apply its truth to today's circumstances. Though not a commentary, it gives valuable insight into the book's message. Though not an introduction, it summarises the important aspects of the book to aid reading and application.

Genesis 1—11
Rebecca Watson
978 0 85746 791 1 £6.99

Psalms
Simon P. Stock
978 0 85746 731 7 £6.99

John
Robert Willoughby
978 0 85746 751 5 £6.99

Colossians and Philemon
Derek Tidball
978 0 85746 730 0 £5.99

brfonline.org.uk

How to encourage Bible reading in your church

BRF has been helping individuals connect with the Bible for over 90 years. We want to support churches as they seek to encourage church members into regular Bible reading.

Order a Bible reading resources pack
This pack is designed to give your church the tools to publicise our Bible reading notes. It includes:

- Sample Bible reading notes for your congregation to try.
- Publicity resources, including a poster.
- A church magazine feature about Bible reading notes.

The pack is free, but we welcome a £5 donation to cover the cost of postage. If you require a pack to be sent outside the UK or require a specific number of sample Bible reading notes, please contact us for postage costs. More information about what the current pack contains is available on our website.

How to order and find out more
- Visit **biblereadingnotes.org.uk/for-churches**.
- Telephone BRF on +44 (0)1865 319700 Mon–Fri 9.15–17.30.
- Write to us at BRF, 15 The Chambers, Vineyard, Abingdon OX14 3FE.

Keep informed about our latest initiatives
We are continuing to develop resources to help churches encourage people into regular Bible reading, wherever they are on their journey. Join our email list at **brfonline.org.uk/signup** to stay informed about the latest initiatives that your church could benefit from.

Subscriptions

The Upper Room is published in January, May and September.

Individual subscriptions
The subscription rate for orders for 4 or fewer copies includes postage and packing:

The Upper Room annual individual subscription   £17.40

Group subscriptions
Orders for 5 copies or more, sent to ONE address, are post free:
The Upper Room annual group subscription   £13.80

Please do not send payment with order for a group subscription. We will send an invoice with your first order.

Please note that the annual billing period for group subscriptions runs from 1 May to 30 April.

Copies of the notes may also be obtained from Christian bookshops.

Single copies of *The Upper Room* cost £4.60.

Prices valid until 30 April 2020.

Giant print version
The Upper Room is available in giant print for the visually impaired, from:

Torch Trust for the Blind
Torch House
Torch Way
Northampton Road
Market Harborough   Tel: +44 (0)1858 438260
LE16 9HL   **torchtrust.org**

THE UPPER ROOM: INDIVIDUAL/GIFT SUBSCRIPTION FORM

All our Bible reading notes can be ordered online by visiting biblereadingnotes.org.uk/subscriptions

☐ I would like to take out a subscription myself (complete your name and address details once)

☐ I would like to give a gift subscription (please provide both names and addresses)

Title .... First name/initials .... Surname ....

Address ....

.... Postcode ....

Telephone .... Email ....

Gift subscription name ....

Gift subscription address ....

.... Postcode ....

Gift message (20 words max. or include your own gift card):

....

....

Please send *The Upper Room* beginning with the January 2020 / May 2020 / September 2020 issue (*delete as appropriate*):

Annual individual subscription ☐ £17.40 Total enclosed £ ....

Method of payment

☐ Cheque (made payable to BRF) ☐ MasterCard / Visa

Card no. ☐☐☐☐ ☐☐☐☐ ☐☐☐☐ ☐☐☐☐

Expires end ☐☐ ☐☐ Security code* ☐☐☐ Last 3 digits on the reverse of the card

*ESSENTIAL IN ORDER TO PROCESS THE PAYMENT

THE UPPER ROOM GROUP SUBSCRIPTION FORM

> **All our Bible reading notes can be ordered online by visiting
> biblereadingnotes.org.uk/subscriptions**

☐ Please send me .... copies of *The Upper Room* January 2020 /
May 2020 / September 2020 issue (*delete as appropriate*)

Title .... First name/initials .... Surname ....

Address ....

.... Postcode ....

Telephone .... Email ....

Please do not send payment with this order. We will send an invoice with
your first order.

Christian bookshops: All good Christian bookshops stock BRF publications.
For your nearest stockist, please contact BRF.

Telephone: The BRF office is open Mon–Fri 9.15–17.30. To place your order,
telephone +44 (0)1865 319700.

Online: biblereadingnotes.org.uk/group-subscriptions

☐ Please send me a Bible reading resources pack to encourage Bible
reading in my church

Please return this form with the appropriate payment to:
BRF, 15 The Chambers, Vineyard, Abingdon OX14 3FE
To read our terms and find out about cancelling your order, please visit **brfonline.org.uk/terms**.

The Bible Reading Fellowship is a Registered Charity (233280)

UR0319

To order

Online: **brfonline.org.uk**
Telephone: +44 (0)1865 319700 Mon–Fri 9.15–17.30

Delivery times within the UK are
normally 15 working days. Prices are
correct at the time of going to press
but may change without prior notice.

Title	Price	Qty	Total
Image of the Invisible	£8.99		
Life with St Benedict	£9.99		
A Fruitful Life (second edition)	£8.99		
Really Useful Guide: Genesis 1—11	£6.99		
Really Useful Guide: Psalms	£6.99		
Really Useful Guide: John	£6.99		
Really Useful Guide: Colossians and Philemon	£5.99		

POSTAGE AND PACKING CHARGES			
Order value	UK	Europe	Rest of world
Under £7.00	£2.00	Available on request	Available on request
£7.00–£29.99	£3.00	Available on request	Available on request
£30.00 and over	FREE	Available on request	Available on request

Total value of books	
Postage and packing	
Donation	
Total for this order	

Please complete in BLOCK CAPITALS

Title .... First name/initials .... Surname..

Address...

.... Postcode ....

Acc. No. .... Telephone ....

Email...

Method of payment

❑ Cheque (made payable to BRF) ❑ MasterCard / Visa

Card no. ☐☐☐☐ ☐☐☐☐ ☐☐☐☐ ☐☐☐☐ ☐☐☐☐ ☐☐☐☐

Expires end ☐☐ ☐☐ Security code* ☐☐☐ Last 3 digits on the
reverse of the card

Signature* .... Date .... / .... / ....
*ESSENTIAL IN ORDER TO PROCESS YOUR ORDER

The Bible Reading Fellowship Gift Aid Declaration

giftaid it

Please treat as Gift Aid donations all qualifying gifts of money made

❑ today, ❑ in the past four years, ❑ and in the future **or** ❑ My donation does not qualify for Gift Aid.

I am a UK taxpayer and understand that if I pay less Income Tax and/or Capital Gains Tax in the
current tax year than the amount of Gift Aid claimed on all my donations, it is my responsibility
to pay any difference.

Please notify BRF if you want to cancel this declaration, change your name or home address,
or no longer pay sufficient tax on your income and/or capital gains.

Please return this form to: BRF, 15 The Chambers, Vineyard, Abingdon OX14 3FE | enquiries@brf.org.uk
To read our terms and find out about cancelling your order, please visit **brfonline.org.uk/terms**.

The Bible Reading Fellowship (BRF) is a Registered Charity (233280)

Transforming
lives and communities

Christian growth and understanding of the Bible

Resourcing individuals, groups and leaders in churches for their own spiritual journey and for their ministry

Church outreach in the local community

Offering two programmes that churches are embracing to great effect as they seek to engage with their local communities and transform lives

Teaching Christianity in primary schools

Working with children and teachers to explore Christianity creatively and confidently

Children's and family ministry

Working with churches and families to explore Christianity creatively and bring the Bible alive

parenting for faith

Visit **brf.org.uk** for more information on BRF's work

brf.org.uk

The Bible Reading Fellowship (BRF) is a Registered Charity (No. 233280)